"**B**efore the adv... erary criticism," says Stephen ... cock, "any form of writing that was supposed to have a laugh in it was called a 'funny piece.' In the days of schoolhouse 'recitations,' Patrick Henry's speech about giving him liberty or giving him death was not recited as a 'funny piece.' But Bret Harte's *Heathen Chinee* was. *Satan's Address to the Sun*, by Milton, was taken either way. So it came about that such expressions as 'to speak a funny piece' or to 'hear a funny piece' became a familiar part of our language, now drifting into oblivion. We now say that the 'distinguished *diseuse* gave a delicious *rendition*,' and that the 'famous impersonator's work showed its usual *brio*' when we really mean that they 'spoke funny pieces.'" Mr. Leacock says in his preface that he can form no better wish for his new book than that it may live up to the old traditions of the "funny pieces" after which it was named.

The book is decidedly a "mixed grill," its contents running all the way from sheer burlesque to little dramatic pieces and essays that almost become serious. But Mr. Leacock is nowhere better than in that peculiar mock scholarship and burlesque of highbrow learning in which, himself a scholar, he has chiefly excelled.

/ 3 /

FUNNY PIECES

FUNNY PIECES

PIECES

A BOOK OF RANDOM SKETCHES

by

STEPHEN LEACOCK

DODD, MEAD & COMPANY
NEW YORK   MCMXXXVI

PRINTED IN THE U. S. A. BY
Quinn & Boden Company, Inc.
BOOK MANUFACTURERS
RAHWAY,   NEW JERSEY

PREFACE

A GENERATION or so ago, the word "pieces" was commonly used to sweep a much wider area than now. It covered practically the whole range of literary, artistic and musical effort. In the "little red schoolhouse" the "entertainment" which antedated such less intense efforts as moving pictures and the radio was made up of "pieces." In the field of oratory a man was said to "speak a piece"—such as the "piece" that Abraham Lincoln spoke at Gettysburg; in art he acted a "piece" (W. Shakespeare wrote some good "pieces" for the schoolbooks); in music he "gave a piece." This made all language of art criticism simple and easy to handle. They didn't say, as we do, that the "maestro" handled the composition with the greatest "brio"; they just said he "played a piece on the fiddle." They didn't say the "charming diseuse gave a delightful character rendition"; not at all, they said "the young lady acted out a funny piece."

That was where the phrase "funny piece" came in. It stood for any performance or any literary production calculated to amuse, in fact almost to make people laugh right out. In the "recitation" book, apart from the "pieces" written for it by W. Shakespeare and by Mr. Addison, and apart from "pieces" taken out of history, there were "funny pieces" such as *'Twas the Night Before Christmas* and *John Gilpin.* In the case of some of the items it was uncertain whether to class them as "funny pieces" or not. *Satan's Address to the Sun,* by John Milton, could be taken either way.

In gathering together the various and varied selections that make up this book, I can form no better wish for them than that they may follow in the tradition set by the "funny pieces" of the past, and meet with the same respectful attention as the old ones did. Their simple character and the obvious personal strain which runs through them disarms unkindly criticism. They are not meant for anything more than they are; they are just "funny pieces."

In one of the pieces below, dealing with an *Interview with a Movie Queen,* I have ventured to borrow from the work of my son, Stephen Leacock, Junior, now beginning to appear in school and college journals.

This book in all is so peculiar in character, so fragmentary and so discursive, that I should not dare to have put it thus together if it were not for the past indulgence of my readers.

STEPHEN LEACOCK.

The Old Brewery Bay,
Lake Couchiching.

TABLE OF CONTENTS

vii

PART III. BRAIN STUFF IN GENERAL

PART IV. NATION AND NATION

PART V. PAPERS OF THE IGNORAMUS CLUB

PART VI. DRAMA SECTION

PART VII. PERSONALIA

PART I

The School Section

Readers who come from the country don't need to be told what a "school section" is. Readers who come from the city don't care what it is. But the name refers to the area which the "little red schoolhouse" swept in the educational sense.

GETTING BY AT COLLEGE

A Study in How to Elude the Examiner

(AUTHOR'S NOTE: *While I was a professor my students used often to ask me whether there was no way to get an education quicker than by the long and arduous route of study and examinations. I always refused to give away the secrets of the profession. But now that I have retired I don't mind explaining that with a little technical skill it is possible to "get by" most of the tests and examinations of school and college.*)

————

EVERY student should train himself to be like the conjurer Houdini. Tie him as you would, lock him in as you might, he got loose. A student should acquire this looseness.

For the *rudiments* of education there is no way round. The multiplication table has got to be learned. They say Abraham Lincoln knew it all. So, too, the parts of speech must be committed to memory, and left there. The names of the Wessex Kings, from Alfred (better Aelfrydd) to his Danish successor Half-Knut, should be learned and carefully distinguished

3

from the branches of the Amazon.

But, these rudiments once passed, education gets easier and easier as it goes on. When one reaches the stage of being what is called a ripe scholar, it is so easy as to verge on imbecility.

Now for college examinations, once the student is let into college, there are a great number of methods of evasion. Much can always be done by sheer illegibility of handwriting, by smearing ink all over the exam paper, and then crumpling it up into a ball.

But apart from this, each academic subject can be fought on its own ground. Let me give one or two examples.

Here, first, is the case of Latin translation, the list of extracts from Caesar, Cicero, etc., the origin of each always indicated by having the word Caesar, etc., under it. On this we seize as our opportunity. The student doesn't need to know one word of Latin. He learns by heart a piece of translated Latin, selecting a typical extract, and he writes that down. The examiner merely sees a faultless piece of translation and notices nothing—or at least thinks the candidate was given the wrong extract. He lets him pass.

Here is the piece of Caesar as required.

These things being thus this way, Caesar although not yet did he not know neither the copiousness of the enemy not whether they had frumentum, having sent on Labienus with an impediment he himself on the first day before the third day, ambassadors having been sent to Vercingetorix, lest who might which, all having been done, set out.

Caesar. Bum Gallicum. Op. cit.

Cicero also is easily distinguished by the cold biting logic of his invective. Try this:—

How now which, what, oh, Catiline, infected, infracted, disducted, shall you still perfrage us? To what expunction shall we not subject you? To what bonds, to what vinculation, to how great a hyphen? Do I speak? Does he? No.

Cicero. In (and through) Catiline.

The summation of what is called the liberal arts course is reached with such subjects as political theory, philosophy, etc. Here the air is rarer and clearer and vision easy. There is no trouble at all in circling around the examiner at will. The best device is found in the use of quotations from learned authors of whom he has perhaps—indeed, very likely—never heard, and the use of languages which he either doesn't know or can't read in blurred writing. We take for granted that the examiner is a conceited, pedantic man, as they all are, and is in a hurry to finish his work and get back to a saloon.

Now let me illustrate.

Here is a question from a recent examination in Modern Philosophy. I think I have it correct or nearly so.

"Discuss Descartes' proposition 'Cogito ergo sum' as a valid basis of epistemology."

Answer:

*Something of the apparent originality of Descartes' dictum, "Cogito ergo sum," disappears when we recall that, long before him, Globulus had written "*TESTUDO ERGO CREPITO," *and the great Arab Scholar Alhelallover, writing about 200 Fahrenheit, has said "*INDIGO ERGO GUM." *But we have only to turn to Descartes' own brilliant contemporary, the Abbé Pâté de Foi Grasse, to find him writing, "*DIMANCHE, LUNDI, MARDI, MERCREDI, JEUDI, VENDREDI, SAMEDI," *which means as much, or more, than Descartes' assertion. It is quite likely that the Abbé was himself acquainted with the words of Pretzel, Wiener Schnitzel and Schmierkäse; even more likely still he knew the treatise of the low German Fisch von Gestern who had already set together a definite system or schema. He writes:* WO IST MEIN BRUDER? ER IST IN DEM HAUSE. HABE ICH DEN VOGEL GESEHEN? DIES IST EIN GUTES MESSER. HOLEN SIE KARL UND FRITZ UND WIR WERDEN INS THEATER GEHEN. DANKE BESTENS.

There—one can see how easy it is. I know it from my own experience. I remember in my fourth year in Toronto (1891) going into the exam room and picking up a paper which I carelessly took for English Philology; I wrote on it, passed on it and was pleasantly surprised two weeks later when they gave me a degree in Ethnology. I had written the wrong paper. This story, oddly enough, is true.

BYGONE SCHOOLBOOKS

I

Mrs. Magnall and Mrs. Marcett

THINGS familiar in daily use never seem queer or odd. Only a retrospect of time or distance can make them so. Thus it is with the tattered schoolbooks that each generation throws around in the classrooms. The torn leaves and the worn backs and the well-thumbed insides are so familiar that they are taken for granted. But after a generation or so they take on an oddity all their own.

There flourished both in England and in America, about a hundred years ago, a type of schoolbook that was all made up of questions and answers. In such books as *Mrs. Magnall's Questions,* and *Peter Parley's Treasury,* the history of all the world and the manners and customs of all its people were thus set forth in question and answer, in searching inquiry and reassuring fact. Thus Mrs. Magnall would ask, "Did not the Roman people claim to descend from Romulus and Remus?" And the answer (written *Ans.*) echoed back: "They did." Mrs. Magnall continued: "Was not the first Roman King of whom we have any authentic account Numa Pompilius?" And the

8

answer reassured her: "He was."

Progress under this system was far more rapid than under the slower methods of today. An intelligent child could scoop up the whole of ancient history almost without effort. The form of the instruction reminds me of the old story of the dialogue carried on, through a speaking tube, between the bartender down below stairs and his boss above. "Is O'Rourke good for two drinks?" "Has he had them?" "He has." "He is."

But behind these books themselves, both for England and for America, there are forgotten chapters of history. Those were the days when Queen Victoria was young, the days before democratic education, when schooling cost money and was beyond the reach —very properly, it seemed—of the poor. Even for many "gentlefolk" the cost of sending children away to school was too high. Many mothers must gather the little flock around their knees and ask, in the words of Mrs. Magnall, "Did not the battle of Salamis put an end to the power of Persia at sea?" and receive the ratifying chorus of assent, "It did."

More even than that. Those were the days when countless English families, of better birth than means, went out to the uttermost ends of the earth, to the "colonies," to build up the British Empire. With them went Mrs. Magnall and Peter Parley. In the backwoods of Upper Canada, in the upcountry of Natal, and in the newer England of New Zealand, the mothers asked their children, "Was not the Assyrian Empire the first of the great Oriental monarchies?" and the children admitted, "It was."

There is something appealing in the naïveté of the yes-and-no system. "Did not the ancient Britons stain themselves with woad?" "They did." No court of law would admit the validity of this as evidence. Any judge would rule it out as a leading question. But the devoted mothers were not a court of law. If there was anything wrong with Mrs. Magnall's method, they never saw it. Indeed, at times the situation was reversed and the pupil in the dialogue, having been content with "yes, yes, yes," for a whole series of questions, suddenly broke out with a perfect coruscation of brilliance, erupting dates, names, and facts with an effulgence that would have dazzled Macaulay. Mrs. Magnall: "What great event happened next in Greece?" *Ans.* "The Peloponnesian War, in which Athens, together with Attica, Boeotia, Locris, Doris, Phocis, Aetolia, and Acharnaria, was leagued against Sparta, Megara, Corinth, together with the Islands of Chios, Romnos, and Samos."

"Was the war of long duration?"

Ans. "This internecine struggle lasted from B.C. 431 till B.C. 404 and witnessed a carnage second only to that of the ravages of the Persians in Cappadocia. In Corinth no less than 2882 houses, 4 temples, and

17 stadii, or open playgrounds of the discoboli, were destroyed in one single assault of the Boeotians."

"Name some of the chief figures of the contest."

"Pericles, Praxiteles, Proxenes, Lysander, Aneximander, Timocles, Themistocles."

After which Mrs. Magnall, completely knocked out, says, "You have answered well. That concludes the history of Greece."

It ought to.

.   .   .   .

Are those questions, you ask, really out of Mrs. Magnall's books? Surely, you say, they were not quite like that? Perhaps not. But that at least is the idea of them. Personally I have not seen them since I was instructed out of them, in the wilds of Upper Canada, sixty years ago.

In the United States, books like *Mrs. Magnall's Questions* had a certain vogue. But the competition of the "little red schoolhouse" and the "grammar school" ran them hard. The question system could only flourish when it got on to a higher ground and into a rarer air than the atmosphere of ordinary education. Exactly this atmosphere and environment were supplied by the newest science of the day, Political Economy. In the era of the middle forties, political economy ranked in authority and certainty second only to divine revelation. To place it within the reach of all the people, little manuals of questions and answers were prepared, of which the most deservedly famous is the one called *Mrs. Marcett's Conversations in Political Economy,* and published in Philadelphia somewhere about 1840.

Mrs. Marcett, as I recall the little book, didn't take part in the conversation herself. She just inspired the book. The dialogue was carried on between a very didactic lady called "Mrs. B" and an infant prodigy called "Caroline." Even a person who has never seen the illustration in the text can picture the two: Mrs. B, in flowing silk and a poke-bonnet, seated, an open book in her hand; Caroline, in pantalettes, standing, her hair parted to a nicety, her face calm and radiant with intelligence. Not Adam Smith nor Ricardo had anything on Caroline.

The dialogue ran along after this fashion:—

Mrs. B: "Is not political economy an important branch of human knowledge?"

Caroline: "It is."

Mrs. B: "Does it not treat of the production of wealth and of its distribution among mankind in the form of rents, profits, interest, and wages?"

Caroline: "It does."

The dialogue so far—Round One—has been all in Mrs. B's favor. But in the next round little Caroline gets back at her in the same way as Mrs. Magnall's inspired child.

Mrs. B: "On what, then, do wages depend?"

Caroline: "On the ratio between population and subsistence—that is to say, on the proportion which the whole number of the workers holds towards the means of subsistence available for their support."

Mrs. B: "Right."

This is pretty feeble of Mrs. B, but she rallies and tries again.

"On what principle of political economy is agriculture governed?"

Caroline has her again.

"By the law of diminishing returns, according to which, after a certain point is passed, any further increment of capital or labor gives a proportionately less return in produce."

This is a knockout. All Mrs. B can say is "Correct."

.   .   .   .

When you come to think about it, there might be a great opportunity to revive this lost method of Mrs. Magnall and Mrs. Marcett. It could be used to impart information on all kinds of current needs. Take for instance the demand in these degenerate days for the revival of the art of mixing drinks, temporarily obscured and nearly lost in America. The services of Mrs. Marcett might be reëngaged to compile a *Mrs. Marcett's Complete Bartender*. Thus:—

Mrs. B: "Is not a cocktail the name of a drink

very commonly taken before dinner for the sake of its power of stimulating and elevating the mind?"

Caroline: "It is."

Mrs. B: "Is not the general basis of a cocktail the admixture of a portion of some ardent or potent spirit—as whiskey, rum or juniper—with a medium calculated to dull the edge of its ardency, such as is vermouth?"

Caroline: "It is."

Mrs. B: "Is not the liquid known as vermouth the *vermis mutis* of the Romans?"

Caroline: "It is."

Mrs. B: "Did the Romans know how to make cocktails out of it?"

Caroline: "They did not."

At about this point very probably Mrs. B's attention wanders and by accident she gets her question in wrong form and so the ball passes to Caroline: thus:—

Mrs. B: "How then is a really first-class cocktail made or combined?"

Caroline: "Take half a wine glass of old Bourbon whiskey and mix it with an equal or slightly lesser portion of French vermouth, the mixture being vigorously shaken up in a closed vessel filled with cracked ice, until such time as the mixture receives a considerable admixture of water drawn from the ice and itself passes into a stage verging on congelation after which it is drained off into funnel-shape glasses."

Mrs. B is down and out.

. . . .

The more you look at it, the more you see how easy it would be to extend this Caroline and Mrs. B stuff into a sort of form or mode application to a thousand kinds of guides and books of instruction. Take an example at random: *Mrs. Marcett's Complete Guide to Harvard*.

Mrs. B: "Is not Harvard a very ancient and honored University?"

Caroline: "It is."

Mrs. B: "Are not some of the lectures given the same as were given 200 years ago?"

Caroline: "They are."

Mrs. B: "May not Harvard, therefore, be compared with the University of Timbuctoo, the College of the Grand Khan at Khiva, the Mosque of El Ashir at Cairo, and the Buried Cities of Yucatan?"

Caroline: "It may."

Compare similarly *Mrs. Marcett's Guide to the New Deal, Mrs. Marcett's Guide to New York,* and opportunities that open up like a field of flowers.

II

Ciphers and Sentiment—The Arithmetic That Was

ONE would look in vain in a modern text-book of arithmetic for anything in the way of fun or sentiment. There is no laughter on the page and the tears are still to fall.

But in reality this only means that all the sentiment, all the heart-to-heart stuff, the imagination that once possessed it, has been purged out. Our arithmetic came to us from the East: and the Oriental people, especially the Hindoos from whom we took it, are nothing if not dreamy or romantic. The Hindoo arithmetic man couldn't think of numbers without putting them into some kind of a personal setting. So when he stated a problem he addressed it as a request to some individual in particular, as for example to a cow—always a sacred creature to the Hindoo, and the very embodiment of ruminating thought. Thus:—

"O cow, standing beside the Ganges, tell me, if thou knowest it, how much is two and then two more?" It appears also that the Hindoo, as a sentimental being, was unable to keep out the idea of "love" or what they call in the movies the "sex motive." He addressed his arithmetic to his sweetheart and presents her with a problem as a sort of love

token.

"Here I bring to you, O Fair One, an isosceles triangle. Tell me, if you love me, whether the angles at the base of it be not equal."

But our arithmetic did not come direct from India. It was imported via Arabia and from the Arabian books translated into mediaeval Latin. This pilgrimage touched it with the colours of mystery that hang around the Kingdom of Haroun al Raschid and the mosques of Mecca and the Grand Cairo. It becomes a first cousin of alchemy and in a way a branch of magic. In fact it was so written up as to give it a queer outlandish touch of mystery and the quaint conceit of a mystic craft.

Listen, thus, to a mediaeval writer of the thirteen hundreds, Thomas of Newmarket, readapting into English a Latin script of Alexander of the City of God. He calls it *The Craft of Nombrynge,* by which he means numbering, and from start to finish he is mighty proud of it. Helping him out a little, but not too much, with his spelling and punctuation we find that he tells us that:—

"This book is called the book of Algorym, or Augrym after lewder folk—" (Just why "augrym" sounded a bit lewd in 1220 A.D. we don't know; we miss the joke.)

"And this book treateth the craft of nombrynge which is also called Algorum." (He said that before,

but time didn't matter in a mediaeval monastery.)
He goes on:—

*"There was a King of Inde, the which hight Alger
and he made this craft."* (One of the Alger boys,
presumably.)

"And after his name he called it Algorym." (That
would seem to follow, but Thomas himself is not
satisfied; he gives a second explanation for good
measure.)

*"Or else another cause is quy it is called Algorym
for the latin word of hit, sic, Algorismus, comes of
Algos, Greek, that is art, latin, craft, English and
rides which is number, latin, number English, and
so it is called Algorismus by addition of this syllable
'mus' and subtraction of d and e."*

(Anybody who doesn't get it now is never going
to get it.) After this we plunge right in:—

*"Furthermore you must understand that in this
craft ben used ten figures as here ben written for
ensample:—0.9.8.7.6.5.4.3.2.1. This present craft is
called Algorismus in the which we use ten signs of
India."*

(Thomas has said this before but he can't bear to
let such a good thing go. But notice what he does
now to brighten it up and say it over again. He puts
it into dialogue):

Quaestio: Why ten figures from India?

Solutio: For as I have said afore they were found first in Inde by a king of that country that was called Algor.

After which, as they say in old French poetry, who doesn't know that doesn't know anything. Meanwhile Thomas of Newmarket drives forward at the same pace to explain, page upon page, what his numbers mean. There is a queer touch of professional pride about it, a consciousness of magic art, especially when he deals with "cifre" of which he is very proud. He says:—

"A cifre tokens nought, but he makes the figure to betoken that comes after him more than he should an he were away and thus one and cifre (10) here by figure of one tokens ten and if the cifre were away and no figure before him he should token but one for then he would stand in the first place. And the cifre tokens nothing himself."

Most of us would admit that, by this time. On goes Thomas. After four more pages he is able to make the proud announcement.

"Here be-gynnes the craft of Addicion."

But we have to remember that time didn't count in the Middle Ages. In point of speed Thomas was rapid to some of those who followed him. Come and walk in the steps of John of Holywood, otherwise Sacrobosco, a long way indeed from California, being presumably Scarborough and certainly "holy." John wrote in the fourteen hundreds a "piece" which he called the *Art of Numbryng,* translated out of Latin into what John understood to be English. The Latin form of the book *De arte numerandi* was one of the earliest books printed and was the principal arithmetic book of the Tudor times.

John of Holywood goes so slowly that he almost falls asleep in his first paragraph:

"Therfore sithen the science" (he means "know that the science") *"of the which at this time we intent to write offstandeth all about number: first we must see what is the proper name therefore and from whence the name came."*

(We know that; Thomas of Newmarket told us two hundred years before.)

"Afterwards what is number, and how many spices of number there been. The name is clept Algorism, had out of Algor, *or of* Algos, *in* Greek, *that is clept in* English *art or craft, and of* Rithmus *that is clept number. So Algorism is clept the art of numbering, or else it is had of* en *or in* and *gogos, that is to say Introduction of Number. And thirdly"*

(Thomas we remember only had two explanations: Holywood has three.)

. . . *"it is had of the name of a king that is clept Algo and Rithmos—so called Algorismus."*

The start is slow. But once John of Holywood got

going he was fairly formidable. He seemed to have more kinds of arithmetic than we do now. He tells us that there are *"nine species of it, numeracioun, addicioun, subtraccioun, mediacioun, duplacioun, multipliacioun, dyvysioun, progressioun, and of Roots the extraccioun."*

It sounds enough.

. . . .

The old writers never could get over the idea that they were being terribly "cute," were imparting a sort of hidden knowledge as from magician to magician. Listen to the author of *Accomptyng by Counters*, reign of Henry VIII, explaining a trick or two to his pupils. To make it lively he puts his book in the form of a dialogue between M and S—master and scholar—the scholar being as simple as Dr. Watson, the biographer of Sherlock Holmes, and as appreciative. *"I perceive numeration,"* says the scholar, meaning that he understands what the figures stand for, *"but I pray you how shall I do in this art to add two sums or more together?"* The master shows him and he is overjoyed. Later on the master puts him on to some real ones. *"One feat I shall teache you,"* he says, *"which not only for the strangeness and secretness is much pleasaunt but also for the good commodity of it right worthy to be well marked. This feat hath been used about 2000 years at the least and yet was it never commonly known, espe-*

cially in English it was never taught yet. This is the art of numbrynge on the hand, with divers gestures of the fingers expressing any sum conceived in the mind."

Can we wonder at the mystery and dignity that to the common eye surrounded learned men four hundred years ago!

.   .   .   .

Thus came arithmetic down the centuries taking on something of the colour of each successive country and century—the dream of the Hindoo, the alchemy of the Arab, the mystery of the mediaeval monastery. Then, as it entered into modern times of trade and industry it reflected the colour of the counting house, the bargain of the shop, the wages of the labourer, the profits of capital: and in the case of an adventurous people like the English, it takes on the magic of the sea, in the computed profits of trading voyages.

Here let us take as our witness a book called *Arithmetic, the Doctrine of Numbers* brought forth in 1749 by a Mr. Solomon Lowe, "Schoolmaster at Hammersmith." Mr. Lowe proves the fact that he lives in a commercial age by writing on his title page a quotation from Addison's *Spectator* which says: *"Numbers are so much the measure of everything that is valuable, that it is not possible to demonstrate the process of any action or the prudence of any under-taking without them."* This is a long way from mystic properties of 7 as the perfect number of the Middle Ages, or the magic squares, or the cunning of the alchemist. This is straight business. Mr. Lowe soon proves it.

"A certain man," he says, *"having driven his swine to the market—viz. hogs, sows and pigs—received 50£. for them, being paid, for every hog, 18 s.: for every sow, 16 s.: for every pig, 2 s."* Mr. Lowe says further that there were as many hogs as sows and for every sow 3 pigs. He wants to know how many were there of each sort?

Most of us would fall down here not knowing the difference between a *hog* and a *pig,* a piece of information which Mr. Lowe fails to give. But at any rate this begins to sound like arithmetic. Mr. Lowe's "problems" have got the real eighteenth-century touch to them. It was the day of hard drinking and even arithmetic got saturated with liquor.

1. *"Four men drink, at table, 16 pennyworth of wine, etc."* (lucky fellows! to get it for 32 cents for the four of them).

2. *"Reduce,"* commands Mr. Lowe in his peremptory way, *"31½ gallons of beer to a fraction of a barrel."* That sounds as if it would take a good deal of drinking.

"*I bought 40 gallons of brandy for 61 8. s.,*" he says, and leaves us too stupefied to ask what happened next. That's only 64 cents a quart.

Try this one:—

"*A brewer,*" says Mr. Lowe, "*mixed 17 gallons of ale at 8.d. per gallon: with 19 gallons at 10.d. per gallon and with 40 gallons at 6.d. per gallon; what,*" he asks, "*is one gallon of this mixture worth?*"

It sounds priceless.

Mr. Lowe's *Arithmetic* recalls to us very vividly the queer state of the criminal law of two hundred years ago.

"*A robbery being committed on the highway,*" he says, in chatting over the art of subtraction, "*there was assessed on a certain hundred*" (that means a country district) "*in the county of York, the sum of £373-14-8: of which the four parishes paid £37-16-4 apiece: the four hamlets £28-3-10: the four townships £19-19 each.*" "*What,*" asks Mr. Lowe, "*was the deficiency?*"—and he tells us, for Mr. Lowe always solves his problems instantly, on the same line, without any waiting, that it was £29-18. But think of the odd system! The hold-up had to be paid for by all the people who lived along the road.

But best of all is the breeze from the salt seas of the English coast that blows the pages of Lowe's book.

"*A ship's company took a prize of 300£. which was to have been divided among them according to their pay and the time they had been on board, etc., etc."*

.   .   .   .

"A captain and 160 sailors took a prize worth, etc."

And here enter into arithmetic those three cele-brated characters A, B and C.

"A, B and C," says Lowe, *"freight a ship for the Canaries."* But he soon has them doing all sorts of other things. *"Three gardeners (A, B and C),"* he tells us, *"have bought a piece of ground."* He gives their names in parenthesis. But he doesn't need to. We would have guessed it was A, B and C. It was just like them to do it.

Before Lowe gets to the end of his book A, B and C already show signs of chasing out all the other characters—the captains, and midshipmen and mer-chants, and brewers and gentlemen, and taking over the arithmetic to themselves.

This, as everyone knows, they presently did, and the other characters, and the distinctive occupations died out.

"A, B and C," says the nineteenth-century arith-metic, "do a certain piece of work." Nor is there any evidence that they shared prize money, or drank fractions of a barrel of beer in return for it.

Thus mathematics lost first its mysticism, then its magic, and finally its romance.

III

Parlez-vous Français?

NEARLY a hundred years ago, when all the world began to go to school and to learn foreign languages, there lived a group of distinguished Frenchmen who probably influenced the minds of foreigners more than all the courts and cabinets of the Kings and Emperors of France. The ideas of foreign nations in regard to France, its institutions and its language, were largely drawn from these men. The greatest names among the group are recognized as those of Ollendorff, Henri Bué and De Fivas. All of them wrote "grammars" with little exercises to show how to turn English into French. All of them, I feel certain from the way they write, were men of distinction. Henri Bué, I should imagine, from the crisp brevity of his sentences, was a general. He says *"Etes-vous là?"* *"Non."* No one but a military man could have grasped the idea so firmly. *"Quelle heure est-il?"* he asks in his abrupt military way; it is the question of a man accustomed to the vigils of war, and knowing what it is to get up at three in the morning.

Ollendorff, there is no doubt, was an unacknowledged member of the royal family, and De Fivas, obviously, in reality the Marquis De Fivas, an aristocrat, all of whose family had perished, or ought to have perished, in the Revolution: or as he himself would have put it in his deeply thoughtful chapter on the Conditional Mood, *"qui eussent voulu qu'ils pussent périr."*

.   .   .   .

Without these men, and their lesser fellows, we should never have understood what we rightly call the genius of the French people. Thus it was for many of us from the pages of Ollendorff and General Henri Bué and the Marquis De Fivas that we learned how fickle the French are, in spite of their heroic qualities, how little their opinions mean, and how rapidly they change their minds.

I take the following conversation, apparently among a little group of French people, otherwise friendly enough, which De Fivas quotes without seeming to see anything wrong with it.

"Speak to him of it!" *"Do not speak to him of it."* *"Give us some of it."* *"Do not give us any of it."* *"Let us tell all the world of it."* *"Do not let us tell anything to anybody!"*

Now what can you do with a people like that? There is no stability, no rest about them. They no sooner start a good idea than they drop it in favour of something else. We can see now of course that it was Baron Ollendorff and the Marquis De Fivas who occasioned the rapid fall of government after government in France, the fall of the Second Empire and the rise of the present Third Republic.

"Let us have a Republic. Do not let us have any (omit any) Republic. Long live the Emperor! Do not let the Emperor live long. Have you any Deputies? No, sir, I have not any (omit any) Deputies."

. . . .

Notice that peculiar use of "omit." That seems to be another national characteristic of the French. They first suggest something eminently reasonable and then calmly say "omit" it. Even General Henri Bué, who deals only in curt military phrases, falls into this fault. He says, "He is without any money (omit *any*)." But why put it in? "Show me," says Ollendorff, "the way to go to the station (omit *to go to*)." But if he's not going there, what is the use in our showing him the way?

This seems again another of the causes of the fatal instability of French government. When the new premier was reported the other day as saying, "Let us first balance the budget," Ollendorff would have whispered to him, "omit *us*": and De Fivas would have instantly added, "Let us not balance the budget."

. . . .

Indeed I cannot but feel that in the case of all these three men the eccentricity of genius reached a point verging on mental aberration. Each one of them seems prepossessed and preoccupied over certain fixed ideas, or rather a certain fixed list of words which they repeat with something very like idiotic obsession.

"Where are the air-holes?" asks Henri Bué: and *"Are there any air-holes (omit any)."* One admits that the plural of air-holes ends in *-aux* whereas you might expect it to end in something else. Perhaps it is because of these little variations that Ollendorff and the rest represent the French as prepossessed with these words. Picture the following ridiculous conversation, taken from De Fivas, and intended, I suppose, to represent intellectual dialogue at a French dinner table!

"Have you the leases of the air-holes?" *"No, sir, but I have the corals and the enamels."*

Then apparently a third person breaks the thread of the discussion with the question, *"Have you seen the stained-glass windows?"* and someone else answers, *"No, but my cousin has bought folding-doors."* Can hopeless inconsistency be carried further?

· · · · · · ·

One is compelled to admit that even the Marquis De Fivas himself at times seems to get utterly disgusted with his own fickle and wayward nation. He pauses in his book, as if in a fit of irrepressible indignation, to put in little lists of their sillinesses under the name of *French Idiotisms* or pieces of French

Idiocy.

Such are:—

To play the devil at four.

To burn to oneself the brain.

To make a crane's leg.

To sleep at a good star, etc., etc.

No other nation but the French, gay, volatile and careless of personal danger, would ever dream of doing these things.

   .   .   .   .

I have always imagined from these and other features of Marquis De Fivas' book that he must have undergone some great sorrow which more or less unhinged, or weakened, his mind. It made him incapable of sustained thought. Again and again he starts an interesting topic, follows it only for a single sentence and then breaks off hopelessly, forgets what he was talking about and begins on something else. If it were not for the evident traces of an original admirable scholarship the effect would be pathetic. This is perhaps best seen when the Marquis is writing in English, for although his chief work is called *French Grammar* a lot of the very best of it is in English. His facility in the language is very great but he shows a certain hesitancy, a reluctance to be quite sure of himself, no doubt owing to the past suffering that had weakened his power of concentration.

Thus he says:—

"*My cousin was born*" (and he adds, "*is born*") "*on the thirteenth of July.*" Then he hesitates again and says, "*the thirteen July.*" Very often he puts in words only to throw them out. "*Give me some bread,*" and then he changes it and says, "*omit some.*" "*Napoleon died at St. Helena in 1821*"; then he thinks better of it and says, "*Napoleon is dead.*" Of course he's dead if he died in 1821.

This peculiar inability on the part of the Marquis to stick to the point is most apparent when he relates historical events. Even from the fragments which he writes one can see that De Fivas once had a splendid historical training. But his inability to sustain any one topic renders it futile.

Thus he starts off with great gusto to tell us all about Alexander the Great. "*Alexander of Macedon,*" he writes, "*called Alexander the Great (or whom one calls Alexander the Great), and who conquered almost the whole world (say, all the world) was the son of King Philip of Macedon and was born in the year B.C. 357.*"

Then, just as he seems to be beginning an interesting biography his mind breaks and he says, "*Diogenes is dead. Diogenes died in the year 323 B.C.*" Then he gets one of his doubtful fits and says, "*Is Diogenes dead? When did Diogenes die?*" Then, apparently forgetting even what he had himself said, he asks: "*Who was Alexander the Great? When was he born?"*

Even with the best intentions it is impossible to follow these discussions. There is not enough continuity. In one case he says, *"Napoleon conquered Europe,"* and then, without a pause, *"Columbus discovered America."*

.   .   .   .

The case of Ollendorff, also, is not without pathos. Poor Ollendorff, like all great dreamers, lived and died among illusions. He thought, as do all true teachers, that his students loved him, that his book fascinated his pupils. In his first preface of 1843 he wrote: *"From the beginning to the end the pupil's curiosity is excited. Each lesson creates a desire for others. . . . Hence,"* he adds triumphantly, *"from one end of the book to the other the pupil's attention is continually kept alive!"* Twenty years later he still thought this. *"The approbation of the public,"* he said, when he put out his ninth edition, was *"his sweet reward."*

Poor Ollendorff! Little did he know that he had been sworn at by a whole generation of schoolboys. But more pathetic still is the oblivion into which he has now fallen and which renders him only a bygone schoolbook.

OPENING DAY AT COLLEGE

An Autumn Study

"WHAT the hell are you taking Divinity for?" asked a bright-eyed co-ed of her companion in the jostling crowd that filled the hall of the Liberal Arts Building on the opening day at college.

"Oh, gee! it's a cinch," answered the other girl, "only two hours a week instead of three and the old bird has never ploughed anyone in thirty years."

"Any prerequisite for it, before you can get in?"

"No, only good moral standing."

"Count me out," said the co-ed.

The crowd jostled on.

At another point in it a fourth-year student greeted the senior professor of English:

"Do you know if the President is back, sir?" he inquired.

"I ain't seen him," answered the professor with quiet dignity.

A little way off in the crowd a group of boys and girls were talking football prospects. "Where in hell is the team?" asked one of the younger girls. "I thought they were going to show up for a practice today."

33

"They were," said the student, "but they went astray in the cars. The feller bringing them up mistook which college they were going to."

"But didn't they know themselves?"

"They knew it's name, but how in the hell would they know where it was!"

"That's right, too," said the co-ed.

And the crowd jostled on, the sombre students and the bright co-eds, moving among one another as aimlessly as bees.

"Say!" said a sophomore to his chum, "I don't seem to see many of the Profs. Don't they usually come back on the opening day? Where's the professor of French?"

"He won't be back for a fortnight, they say. He's over in Paris learning French."

"What's he need that for?"

"Search me."

"And where's that fat feller that lectures us on dietetics?" "Still at a summer school, giving a course on overeating."

At one side of the crowd near to the entrance a tall dignified man moved along the hall. The students parted to let him through in silence.

"Who's that?" asked a freshman.

"That's the Dean of the Faculty." A minute or two later they saw the crowd parting again and heard all through the hall loud calls and exuberant greetings of "Hullo, Bill!" "How are you, Bill?" "Hurray for Bill!"

"And who's that?" asked the Freshman.

"That's Bill Jingleman, the Janitor."

And the crowd jostled on.

RECOVERY AFTER GRADUATION

How Fatal Is a College Course?

IT is very commonly supposed, or taken for granted, that a man comes out of college with his mind hopelessly impaired. I do not think that this is so. I have known a great many cases of recovery, which, if not absolutely complete, seemed at least permanent.

More than that. If a man will set himself to preserve what he has gained at college, he will find that, as he grows old, he is able in his leisure to fall back upon his education as a delightful *reductio ad absurdum*.

I know a case in point. Most boys at school have at some time learned all the dates of the Saxon and Norman kings. But as a rule they fail to keep this up, and lose all the good of it. I have an old friend, a college graduate, who has carefully kept this knowledge alive. He is now able in his old age to get great enjoyment from saying over these dates to himself. His keepers say that he shows many other signs of mental activity, and often recites for them lists of genitive plurals and verbs that take the dative.

How different with most of us! We all remember that the prepositions *ad, con, in* and *inter* govern something—but just *what*, eludes us. We are there-fore unable to apply the knowledge gained. You and I perhaps once knew that the genitive of *supellex* (furniture) was *supellectilis*. But later on when we came to furnish a house and could have used this information, it had slipped away. Horace puts it very well in his usual wistful way—but I forget just how.

I am not referring to the classics alone. The diffi-culty seems to appear all along the line. How much our college mathematics ought to mean to us, if we only kept them clean and bright, like a sword ready to be drawn from the scabbard. Take the logarithm. I suppose no more powerful implement of human ad-vance was ever fashioned than when Montesquieu dis-covered the logarithm—I think it was Montesquieu. *"The logarithm of a number to a given base is the index of the power to which the base must be raised to produce the given number."* The old fellow hit the mark right in the centre first time.

But for most of us this bright instrument is use-less. We have forgotten how to raise the base. Had we kept any reasonable recollection of second-year hydraulics the thing would be easy. But no! There is the base and we can't lift it.

Yet it pleased me, I must say, at my country place last summer when there was some mathematical diffi-culty about marking the tennis court to find one of my guests, a student in my classes at McGill, offer to work out the measurement of the court with a logarithm. He said it was quite simple. He needed, in short, nothing but an hypotenuse and two angles, both of which luckily were found round the place. It was very interesting to watch the boy calculating at first. I am certain that he would have got his solution, only while he was preparing to mark the court by means of his logarithm the chauffeur marked it with whitewash.

It may be said that mathematics is, for most of us, a thing apart. Not all of us have the knack of my McGill student. But where we all show the greatest shortcomings in our education is in the matter of our studies in English literature—the very language and thought of our nation. Here I am afraid it is only too true that our college methods fall short of what one could wish.

I am thinking especially of poetry. I fear it is an undeniable fact that poetry is dealt with, by our literature teachers, in exactly the same way as a compound of gases is treated in the chemistry department. It is broken up, analysed, labelled, examined, and finally reduced to the form of solid matter.

Let me take as an example a well-known stanza of which the melody and the pathos, even after a professor has done his worst with it, still linger in the mind.

The boast of heraldry, the pomp of power,
  And all that beauty, all that wealth e'er gave,
Awaits alike th' inevitable hour:—
  The paths of glory lead but to the grave.

Now follows the professorial analysis:—

Boast. How do you distinguish boast from boost? Would it be an improvement to say, "The boost of heraldry." If so, why?

Heraldry. What is the Greek for this?

All that beauty. Question:—all what beauty?

Awaits. What is the predicate and what is predicated?

Lead but to. What is the difference between *but to* and *but in?* Which is preferable here?

Final Question. Write of the life of the poet Gray, being particular to remember that his grandfather was born in Fareham, Hants, or possibly in Epsom, Salts.

Somehow one feels that this is not quite satisfying. For many of us indeed a number of the greatest masterpieces of literature are forever hopelessly damaged by our having studied them in a literature class. I recall here particularly Tennyson's wonderful verses, written just at the close of his life, waiting to "cross the bar," his wearied eyes looking out already from his seaside home in the Isle of Wight to horizons infinitely far.

Twilight and evening star
And one clear call for me,
And may there be no moaning of the bar
When I put out to sea.
But such a flood as, moving, seems asleep,
Too full for sound and foam
When that which drew from out the boundless deep
Turns again home.

These verses seem to me the last word in poetry, the absolute proof of the sublimity of its reach—beyond prose. Our measured life is pictured in the moving flood, moving never to return.

But I have never felt that my appreciation of the poem—which appeared in my college days—was heightened by the notes I took on it in class. I have them still. They read:—

Twilight. At what time is it twilight in Hampshire in June?

Evening Star. Explain this phenomenon and show there is nothing in it.

Moaning of the bar. How was the bar regulated in Tennyson's time?

But yet all this doesn't mean that education is futile and thrown away. What happens really depends upon a man's self. If, after graduation, he sits down and broods over his education, why, naturally it will impair his mind. But it is his duty to be up and doing when he leaves college, forget all about his education, act as if he never had any, cultivate bright thoughts and cheerful ideas and he will soon find himself on the level of those about him.

Then as time goes on, more and more he will acquire that comfortable feeling that after all he has got in his education a *pons asinorum* that no one is going to take away from him.

good

HISTORY REVISED

Famous Old Stories Restored to Their Proper Setting

I. COLUMBUS AND THE EGG

How many of the famous stories and anecdotes of history have become hopelessly damaged in the telling. Very often the whole point of the story has been revised. Take the familiar story of Christopher Columbus and the egg. Everyone has read how Columbus rebuked the envy of the Spanish courtiers at his discovery of America by asking them to balance an egg on one end. When they failed to do it, Columbus dinted the egg at one end and it stood balanced; all that was needed was to think of it first. So the story is told.

But that was not what happened at all about America and the egg. It was the other way around. Here is the true story:

Christopher Columbus on his return to Spain in 1492 was invited to a banquet by King Ferdinand and Queen Isabella. It was really just a chance invitation, owing to some tale of his having found a new desert island. But he was honoured by being seated between the royal consorts. The talk falling on

America and how he happened to get the idea of discovering it, Columbus turned modestly to Queen Isabella and said, "I'll show you; could you lend me an egg for a minute?"

"What for?" interjected the king.

"I'll show you," said Columbus, "just let me have an egg."

The queen beckoned to the Chamberlain of the Palace.

"Fetch Admiral Columbus an egg," she said.

The Chamberlain whispered in the queen's ear.

"No," said the queen, "bring one out of the cold storage."

The egg was brought.

Columbus rolled up his sleeves.

"Now you see," he said, "I have nothing up my sleeve."

"Wait," said the king, "lift your arms up off the table. All right. Go ahead."

Columbus held up the egg.

"Do you see this egg?"

"We do," echoed all the guests.

"You observe it is just an ordinary egg-shaped egg?"

"It is," said the guests.

"Now I suppose," continued Columbus, "that it would not be possible to make it stand up on one end!"

"No!" cried all the crowd.

"Well, I can do it," said Columbus.

"Gracious!" sniggered the queen, "how could you possibly do that? It will fall over."

"Watch me," said the Genoese.

Holding the egg firmly between his thumb and finger, Columbus gave it a smart knock against the table, so as to dint the shell at one end. After that he put it up on the broken end where it remained standing.

A burst of admiration swept the table.

"Fetch him more eggs!" said the king.

Columbus stood up six eggs one after the other.

The wonder and admiration of the courtiers knew no bounds.

All that evening and the next day the king kept Columbus smashing eggs and standing them up. The news spread through the kingdom. The *Royal Gazette* of Castille and Aragon next morning carried a news item: "Make egg stand up. Wonderful trick performed by Admiral C. Columbus." Editorially the paper said: "While we are not inclined to attach much importance to the alleged discovery by Admiral Columbus of a large island east of the Azores, we recognize in his egg trick one of the finest exploits of Italian inventiveness. It will certainly help to put

Madrid on the map as the third, if not the second, egg-centre east of Constantinople."

People at the court and in the clubs talked of nothing but the egg trick. "I saw a man," said one, "do a perfectly wonderful trick with an egg—a fellow called Christopher Columbus."

"Really," replied another, "I wonder if that is the same Christopher Columbus who started that fool story about a desert island called America."

In a short time the egg trick acquired such celebrity that the king decided that there might be something in the yarn about the island. A new expedition was sent out and returned with the news there really was a large island, possibly even a continent, at the place indicated. The result was the United States.

But to his contemporaries Columbus always remained known as the man who invented the egg trick. It was much the harder thing to do.

II. WOLFE AND GRAY'S "ELEGY"

All of the schoolbooks narrate also the famous story of General Wolfe and the reading of Gray's "Elegy," the night before the taking of Quebec. As told in the history books it runs as follows:

"As the boats made their way slowly and silently, with muffled oars, against the current of the river in the gathering dusk, one of the officers, standing in Wolfe's boat, read aloud from a new poem just arrived from England, the immortal stanza of Gray's "Elegy."

> *"The boast of heraldry, the pomp of power,*
> *And all that beauty, all that wealth e'er gave,*
> *Awaits alike th' inevitable hour.*
> *The paths of glory lead but to the grave."*

"Gentlemen," said General Wolfe to his officers, "I would rather have written those lines than take Quebec tomorrow."

So runs the orthodox version. But as a matter of fact it is absolutely incorrect. It has got the whole business exactly backward. What really happened was like this. The officer began to read:

> *"The boast of heraldry—"*

"Did you say 'the boast of heraldry,' " interrupted Wolfe, "or the 'boost of heraldry'?"

" 'Boast,' " said the officer and resumed:

> *"The boast of heraldry, the pomp of power,*
> *And all that beauty—"*

"All what beauty?" said Wolfe.

"It says 'all *that* beauty,' " said the officer.

"All that beauty, all that wealth e'er gave,
Awaits alike th' inevitable hour.
The paths of glory lead but—"

"How could they 'lead but,'" exclaimed Wolfe, "it must be *'boot.'*"

"No," said the officer, "it isn't. It says, 'lead but.'"

"Well, gentlemen," said the general, "all I can say is that I'd rather take Quebec tomorrow than have written that poem."

III. KING ALFRED AND THE CAKES

Another much misunderstood episode of history is the famous story of the Saxon King Alfred and the cakes. It is told as follows:

King Alfred at the critical moment of his fortune entered in disguise the home of a poor peasant woman. There he sat down in pensive thought. "While you are sitting there," said the woman, "kindly keep your eye on these cakes in the oven so that they don't burn." With that the woman went out. When she returned, Alfred was still sitting lost in thought, the cakes burned to a crisp. When reproached by the woman he admitted that he was the king.

Such is the original story which obviously has no point at all. It leaves out all that happened after. The woman told all her neighbors that the king was so absent-minded that he let the cakes burn. The thing got into the papers, "King Deep in Thought Burns Cakes," "Absent Alfred Destroys Dough," "Sedentary Saxon Burns Buns," "Meditating Monarch Jeopardises Johnny-cake," etc., etc.

In short, the thing went all over. It was the biggest "Ad" that any king had had for years. It started an "Alfred Boom" that soon had nation-wide reactions. Within a month Alfred the Saxon was offered the nomination of the Heptarchy. In the ensuing campaign, burnt cakes were carried aloft by enthusiastic Alfredites.

It was not till after his crowning victory at the battle of Hastings that Alfred admitted he had done it on purpose.

THE MERIT OF THE YOUNG

If Our Teachers Could Only Discern It

IT is in these bright autumn days of early fall that all the colleges and the high schools, and even the little red schoolhouses on the crossroads, hold what they call Commencement Exercises. At these gatherings all the prizes are handed out for last year's work, and speeches are made over all the bright little boys who have carried off the prizes.

It has been my lot to listen to an uncounted number of these speeches, delivered by the principal of the school, or by the chairman of the trustees or the head of the school board or some other such functionary. The little boys who are to receive the prizes are lined up in a row; their faces are bright and eager; their eyes are full of intelligence. Study? Why, those boys couldn't stop studying if they tried to. Come first in the class? Why, where else would any of those boys come? Medal for good conduct? Most certainly, what else could a boy with a face like that do but behave himself?

But it has always seemed to me that the schools give the prizes and the medals to the wrong lot of boys. To me merit lies elsewhere.

49

Listen to this. Here is the sort of speech that the chairman of the school trustees ought to be making at such a gathering.

AWARD OF THE ALGEBRA PRIZE

"Now, ladies and gentlemen, I want to present the first prize in Algebra to Master Willie Nut. Stand up, Willie, and try to lift your head if you can. Don't shuffle with your feet; no one is going to strike you; you are going to get a prize. This boy Willie, ladies and gentlemen, has now been three years at Algebra and he still does not know the difference between a and b. After three years of strenuous exertion Willie does not know that a *plus* b is greater than a *minus* b, and is unable to add $2x$ *plus* $3x$ *plus* $4x$. And yet for three years, this boy came to class every day and sat there uncomplaining. For three years, day after day, no gleam of comprehension ever broke upon his mind as to what it was all about. Those bright little pups who were presented to you for medals earlier in the afternoon sat in their class, happy, absorbed and comprehending. It needed no merit on their part to work at Algebra. Not so Willie Nut. Willie's brain, ladies and gentlemen, had come straight down to him without a single break or alteration from the Stone Age. If you will look at Willie, you will see that the conformation of his little head is that of what is called by biologists the Homo Sapiens, or human being, as op-posed to Pithecoid Ape. No, ladies and gentlemen, Willie is not an ape. But he had a close run for it. And so he sat there in the Algebra class, uncomprehending and uncomplaining. They beat him up and he never struck back. They detained him after four and he crawled out home in the dusk, still uncomplaining. He took it as his natural lot. No joy or interest, ladies and gentlemen, ever illuminated the studies of Willie Nut. But he didn't quit. He was still there. On his school reports they marked the words—'bad,' 'awful,' 'hopeless,' but he went right on.

"Have you ever seen, ladies and gentlemen, the great French piece of sculpture by Rodin called *The Thinker?* Perhaps not. It is the figure of a primitive man, seated, his great frame bowed in concentrated thought, his small head sunk upon his hand—some simple gleam of a first effort of the intellect has come to him; some dream of numbers, of adding and subtracting, has dawned upon his mind and he will not let it go.

"That figure straight through the ages is Willie Nut. He can't learn Algebra; he never will, but he will take this prize (Come forward, Willie, to receive it; don't try to be graceful; you can't; just reach out your nervous hand into the unseen air); he will take this prize for Algebra and go forth in life and he will succeed. He will succeed, ladies and gentlemen, as these bright young creatures never will.

Some day when they are what are called leading lawyers and captains of business, Willie here will be, let us say, the janitor of an apartment building or the night watchman of a bank—honest, honoured and respected. He will be able to sit and read his evening paper—nearly all of it—to himself, at any rate, if not aloud. He will be able to work figures (add tons of coal), to write down telephone numbers, and, if he has to, write a short note or even a letter. His achievement, ladies and gentlemen, will be greater, proportionately, than that of any boy in the class, because he has got in him that steady, persistent unconscious staying power that has lifted mankind above the apes!

"Here, Willie, take your prize—stop—he's fallen off the platform. Never mind, here's your prize anyway, Willie."

.   .   .   .

And when Willie Nut has sat down, or fallen down, or vanished, let us make a second call and present

THE MEDAL FOR GOOD CONDUCT

For this our chairman may speak in terms such as the following:

"And now it is my pleasant duty to present the Gold Medal for Good Conduct, which is awarded this year to Johnnie Tough. Stand up, Johnnie, and let them see you. A pretty hard-looking tough lot, is he not—in external appearance?

"This boy Johnnie Tough, ladies and gentlemen, has been regarded by a painful misunderstanding, which I am here to correct, as the Bad Boy of the School. I am willing to admit that there was a certain basis for such a reputation. It was Johnnie Tough, you will remember, who received a thrashing last year for placing a bent pin on the school inspector's chair. At the time of his licking the hope was expressed by the presiding authorities at the performance that he would repent. He has not.

"It was this same boy who put the cayenne pepper on the school stove, who let loose a cat in the geography class, and who imitated the crowing of a rooster during the school inspector's speech on the progress of education.

"Johnnie Tough, I gather, has broken all the rules laid down by the school board. He is not only a thoroughly bad boy, as instanced already, but he is in addition a hardened liar. When asked who broke the glass in the fan light in Class Room No. 2 he answered, 'I don't know.' Later he told his friends that he did it, but that he wasn't going to be fool enough to say so.

"It is a matter of common knowledge that Johnnie Tough possesses an automatic pistol and that he has been heard to say that he has half a mind to shoot up the geography teacher.

"Matters came to a climax last week, ladies and gentlemen, when Johnnie Tough was found smoking an elm-root cigarette in the school corridor. For this he was expelled.

"But I have now the pleasure of summoning him back to the school and awarding to him, as a worthy recipient, the Gold Medal for Good Conduct.

"Do you not realize, ladies and gentlemen, that this is the kind of boy that makes a nation? These other anaemic little pups couldn't break a rule if they tried. They haven't got enough stuff in them to do it.

"But this Johnnie Tough, beaten, degraded and expelled, smashing the rules, shooting up the teachers, smoking elm-root and working hard to acquire profanity—this is a real boy. Later on in this nation's history, Johnnie will turn up somewhere—anywhere where danger is—high in an aeroplane, or under the sea, or in the thick smoke of battle—fierce and fearless—that is the destiny of Johnnie Tough. He will die one of the nation's heroes, one of that noble group of tough boys who turned into great men.

"Here, Johnnie, take your medal and run along and shoot the geography teacher if you feel like it. We can spare him."

CAMPUS NOTES

When the Methods of Commerce and Athletics
Obtain a Still Further Hold on the Colleges

RUMOUR has it that Yale will probably sell Professor Smith to Harvard. If the deal goes through, this will be the fourth man bought from Yale by Harvard this year.

———

A work-out of the Notre Dame Theological Debating Team was tried last Sunday. Several of the divinity men are shaping up well and various offers have been made to buy the entire lot. Among other prospective buyers is the New York Rationalist Institute.

———

Professor Hickstein, the physicist, has jumped his bond and will go to the University of Pittsburgh. His lawyers say that if he is willing to forfeit the bond Columbia has no way of holding him.

———

The serious difficulties that prevented the delivery of Professor Clutch's great moral lecture on *Denial of Self as a Moral Factor* have now been removed and the lecture will be put on in the Megatherium Auditorium at an early date. It is understood that the

Professor will accept a fifty-fifty split of the box office receipts instead of the sixty-forty originally asked, but will keep the original sixty-forty on the broadcast.

———

Tuscahoma University has made a big scoop in buying the bones of Robert Burns from the town council of Dumfries. The secretary of the college in an interview yesterday said, "Tuscahoma needs tradition. These bones will go a long way toward making it. All our boys are delighted. They claim that Burns' bones are always ahead of the Dinosaur bones which Chicago got from Central Mongolia. They say they are better bones."

———

It was announced yesterday that Roquefort College is proposing to sell its French Department at rock bottom figures. The college executives claim that they can lay in Spanish at fifty per cent of the cost. "There is very little money in French just now," declares the President. "The demand is very dull and the interest is not enough to keep up the overhead. We lost heavily last year in our courses on the French Classical Drama."

PART II

The Literary Section

WHAT THE REVIEWERS MISSED

If they had only had a chance at the Masterpieces of the Past!

(NOTE. *Every author knows what wretched fellows the book reviewers are!*
—*Their patronizing air of knowing everything, eh!*
—*their terrific assumption of scholarship!*
—*their pretense that they understand and use all foreign languages!*
—*their way of reviewing a book by talking about something else altogether different!*
—*their confusion of misprints with mistakes of fact!*
—*their insistence that somebody else said the same thing much better years and years ago!*
—*their perpetual moan that the author's powers are failing and that his latest book shows a terrible falling off—looks like paresis!*
—*We know them, don't we, boys?*

And most of all their latest trick of reviewing the book not under its own title but under a fool heading made up by themselves with the real one printed at the foot of the page.

59

So, just to get back at them, here are a few samples of the way in which they would have got to work on a few of the world's great books of the past.)

I

AN OLD CAMPAIGNER'S LOG.* *New Volume of Memoirs on Savage Life in the British Isles.*

> And down below appears:—
> * Bellum Britannicum. Julius Caesar. Rome (N. Y.?). $1.50.

Readers who were fascinated with the high adventure and rollicking fun of General Julius Caesar's first work, the *Bellum Gallicum,* will rise from the perusal of this second book of memoirs with a feeling of disappointment—if they can rise at all. We ourselves are free to confess that we were not only disappointed but practically disgusted, a state into which we easily get over an author's second volume. We said to ourselves as we read it: "The touch is no longer the same"—*Il tocco mon è più il mismo.* We said it ourselves in Italian, but for the poor nuts, our readers, we have to say it in English.

Here and there in the *Bellum Britannicum* we catch again something of the fun of its lively predecessor. There is a laughable picture of the tenth legion reaching the coast of Sussex, missing the wharf and having to jump into the water—which turned out to be up to their necks! This is comedy indeed!

But for the most part the pages are dullness itself with none of the power of simple and vivid presentation for which we looked in vain. We can always find something to look in vain for, if we look hard enough. The truth is that General Caesar is not equipped for the discussion of savage life. He would have done well to prepare himself for his task by making the acquaintance of such books as Catlin's *North American Indians,* or Mr. Morton's *Walks in Wales.* But even at that, there is much to which the archaeologist will take exception at every step. In reading the highly unsatisfactory account of the Druids, we felt ourselves compelled to wonder whether General Caesar had ever read Confucius! If so, he would know that what he took for "woad" is wood alcohol. We even wonder, in reading the very confused account of the campaign against the Iceni, whether the author had ever read Jomini's *Campaigns of Napoleon* or *With Lee in Virginia.* If not we'll send them to him.

Nor can we endorse the rather cramped and unvaried style used by the general. His use of the ablative absolute, amusing at first, grows wearisome. Again and again he uses the pluperfect conditional passive when the more correct thing to use—the only fair thing to use—would be the gerund, or, at best, the supine. The general, as a writer, is sadly lacking in variety of expression, in synonyms. He calls the soldiers on each and every occasion "*milites*," instead of varying the term, as, for example, Mr. Polybius does, by calling them also "*combattentes*," "*nostri pueri*," or "*the boys in blue*." It's a pity that General Caesar never had a training in journalism; indeed it is a pity he ever wrote at all; we might almost say it is a pity he was ever born.

Apart from that we welcome him to the ranks of our Roman literature.

P.S. We forgot to say that the book is disfigured by a number of distressing misprints, such as "Londinium" for "London," "vallum" for "valley," and "usque" for "whiskey."

II

NEW TEXT ON STATE GOVERNMENT.* Our Politicians as Seen by a College Professor.

And down below:—
* The Prince. Nicolas Machiavelli. Florence (Kansas?). $1.98.

Professor Machiavelli has previously earned a very considerable reputation as the author of the learned

Discorsi, which reputation we fear will not be enhanced by the present volume. *The Discorsi*—which we prefer to call *Discorsi* and not Discourses because we know Italian—bore the distinct mark of a *maestro,* and, if even only on the surface, reflected something of the *chiaro-oscuro* of the glory of the *cinquecentisti.* The present volume, we fear, will meet none of the success of its predecessor. Its very name, the *Prince,* is misleading, so much so that even we ourselves don't get it. But the worst fault of the book is its obvious lack of moral enthusiasm which unfits it for any general use in colleges. Professor Machiavelli is an Italian, and that, for us, will account for any quantity of personal depravity. But he is much mistaken if he thinks that the wives and mothers of this country will tolerate a work of this sort in the *curricula* of our *collegia,* or even in the *arcana* of our *cenabula.*

We have no wish to excite race prejudice. Professor Machiavelli may be a skunk or he may not, we are not raising the question. We are leaving it where it is. But we cannot help but wonder whether Professor Machiavelli ever read Smiles' *Self Help,* or Louisa Alcott's *Little Women,* or Mr. Slopover's *Ministering Children?* We feel that had he done so he would have been a different man, in fact less Italian. There are numerous misprints in the book.

Among other errors is the spelling of the author's name with one c; we spell it with two.

III

RAISING HELL. Pen Pictures of Battles *in the* Sky.

> And down below:—
> * Paradise Lost. John Milton. London (Ontario?). $1.00.

If Mr. Milton had seen *The Birth of a Nation* or Noel Coward's *Cavalcade* (we don't know that he did not), he would have had a better idea of handling the wide canvas which he so ambitiously attempts to fill. As a writer of pleasant little lyrics and in his chats on the liberty of the press, the right of divorce and other lighter topics of the hour, Mr. Milton has shown himself not without a pleasant fancy and a happy gift of expression—what Horace has called a *curiosa felicitas* (a thing we can appreciate because we know Latin). But this large picture is beyond his power. Quite frankly his "paradis" lacks interest, lacks those peculiar elements without which, to us, even paradise would not be paradise. The attempt to produce a scene of that sort without an adequate singing and dancing chorus is always doomed to

failure. Even admitting the charm of the conversations in paradise, as reported by Mr. Milton, in regard
to fixed fate, free will, foreknowledge absolute, we
venture to think that either Dewey, or Royce or
Rolls presents a far better discussion of the points
involved. The character of the Snake presents an
excellent touch of incidental wit badly needed in a
dull volume.

There are the usual number of unfortunate misprints, such as "God," for "Gawd," "Adam" for
"Adams," etc., etc.

IV

THE NATURE MAN SPEAKS. * *Open-air Book
for Thoughtful Minds.*

> And down below appears:—
> * Principia Philosophiae Naturalis. Sir Isaac
> Newton. London and Johannesburg. $3.00.

Sir Isaac's work appears most opportunely just at
the opening of the gardening season, when nothing
is so agreeable as to pass the idle hours in the pauses
of one's work with the open-air perusal of a volume
suited to the time and place. These principles of
natural philosophy are admirable pabulum for the
nature lover—which reminds us that we saw a pair
of orioles at the foot of our garden yesterday, the

first of the brilliant little fellows to make their summer appearance. We tiptoed down our garden path in the hope of a nearer view, but the little love-pair caught sight of us, and at the very first sight they uttered a loud and apprehensive "tweet, tweet"! and were off again at full speed for the south. Sir Isaac would have loved an oriole as much as we do. We were all the more sorry to lose them insomuch as yesterday witnessed our first gathering of a mess of garden peas, an event nearly always simultaneous with the orioles' taking up their sojourn with us. However, we will hope it will not be a case of *au revoir* but that they will come back. The green peas we grow are the Tarantula, the large firm bulbous pea with the huge pod, such as Sir Isaac would have liked. We plant them early in the snow, just as we think Sir Isaac did. So at least we gather from the illustrations and diagrams in his "natural philosophy," which we understand to be plans of a garden—if they are not, we don't know what they are.

Sir Isaac's book unfortunately contains a number of typographical errors—due no doubt to the increasing difficulty of setting Latin type in our English printing houses. Thus we find repeatedly "hoc" an evident misprint for "hock" and "hic" instead of the more usual "hick," and "sol" evidently intended for "solus," the sun; "octo!" for "right, oh!", etc., etc.

V

SOCIETY IN ITS SIMPLEST TERMS.* *French Writer Analyses the Giddy Throng.*

And down below:—
* Le Contrat Social. J. J. Rousseau. Paris (Kentucky?). $1.40.

Monsieur Rousseau—we call him Monsieur because to us French is a second language and almost a third —writes extremely well. His *livre* lacks something of the quality of the other *livres* which he wrote before, but that is only to be *expecté*. Indeed, as one says in French, *tout change,* or, as the witty Abbé Fénélon cleverly expressed it, *Toutes les choses ont une fin,* a phrase impossible to translate, as everything is in witty French. Monsieur Rousseau in his *Contrat Social* conducts us at once into a *milieu sauvage,* an expression so difficult to convey in English that we won't even try to. He finds the basis of this—the *base* so to speak—to be the principle of *liberté* (*principe de la liberté*) freely accepted among men (*hommes*). To this first principle he adds that of *égalité* (or, roughly speaking, equality) and then very ingeniously connects the two of them with *fraternité*. By putting the three together he reaches the combined idea (*idée*) of *liberté, égalité, fraternité*. After that such secondary ideas as *paternité, maternité, qualité, jollité*, etc., etc., follow of themselves. In short, as with all works of real genius, the thesis once started runs of itself.

Our only doubt, the only question which we raise, is whether Mr. Rousseau was acquainted with the Declaration of Independence. He makes no mention of it. But if he had stopped to peruse even the opening preamble he would have seen his own ideas reflected—I shall be wicked enough to say, anticipated—in an almost incredible fashion.

Even if he did not know about the Declaration of Independence, we cannot but ask had he heard of the Edict of Nantes, and of the Massacre of St. Bartholomew. And what about the Magna Carta?

It is the duty of the critic to submit everything to a rigorous and impartial examination. We suspect that Monsieur Rousseau has drawn from a number of authorities, including certainly St. Thomas Aquinas, whom he refrains from naming. This, however, does not prevent his *livre* from having a great *intérêt* and a considerable *mérite*. If not exactly what one might call *une livre de poche* or *un volume de pantalon* it can at least be classed as an *essai de pyjamas*—a thing we won't even try to put into English.

There are, of course, a number of misprints, such as "égalité" for "equality" and so forth.

VI

NEW LIGHT ON WATERLOO. *French Novelist Retells Story of Battle.*

> And down below:—
> * Les Misérables. Victor Hugo. Paris (Ontario?). $2.25.

Monsieur Hugo—we pronounce his name "Uggo," with a very short double g, difficult for our readers to say—in his new volume of fiction offers an ambitious attempt to reconstruct the Battle of Waterloo. Of the story itself, *Les Misérables,* we need say little except that it held our attention—a difficult thing to do. Mr. Hugo, whose earlier works showed undoubted genius, unfortunately betrays that flagging power which at once attends literary success. Quite frankly he is not what he was. Nor do we think he ever will be. But we especially wished that he had left Napoleon alone. We ourselves understand Napoleon but we doubt if anyone else does. The unceasing stream of books and memoirs in regard to the *First Empire* (that is what we call it; our readers will get it if they try), bears evidence to the sustained public interest in the career of the Great Corsican (one of our names for Napoleon; he came from Corsica). It is no hesitation to say that his footsteps have literally been followed from Ajaccio to Porte Ferraio and his personal contacts from the days of Paoli to those of Pozzo di Borgo (no one gets this but ourselves). Yet we could wish that writers would desist from any further attempts at an analysis of Napoleon's motives. We know them, of course, but no one else does. We fathom exactly this attitude at the Congress of Rastadt and we get his ideas at the Conference of Chantillon, but who else ever heard of those places? Mr. Hugo's presentation of Napoleon as a wearied Titan is one which we cannot accept. Not that we don't know what a Titan means. It isn't that. We do. But we claim that he was not wearied—"tired," if one will, "fatigued," if we must, "exhausted," if one has to, or if you like "bust"—but not wearied. Very probably Mr. Hugo wouldn't get the difference.

Mr. Hugo is on more solid ground in his presentation of the Battle of Waterloo. His graphic picture of the *terrain* as represented by a capital letter A, is one which we accept at once. It is vivid, brilliant, and quite within Mr. Hugo's scope. But the letter A is about as far as he gets. The tactics of the battle—and when we say "tactics" we mean "tactics," not mixing it up with "strategy" as our readers do—are not grasped by Mr. Hugo. He does not realize that Napoleon's fatal error (we saw it at once) was in not throwing back his left so far that it would smack against his right and then basing himself obstinately with his rear well elevated toward the Prussians. His failure to do this led to the tragedy of St. Helena (St. Helena was where they sent him). Nor can we blame the English for refusing to him the rôle of Themistocles (Themistocles is the rôle they refused him).

Mr. Hugo's French we find clear, accurate and free from grammatical error. Without calling him a *savant* we feel that he is quite *au courant* with the use of past subjunctives and other difficulties which bother even us.

VII

.   .   .   .

And yet sometimes the reviewer finds something of his own size, something he can really get enthusiastic about. As witness below:—

DARWINIAN THEORY REFUTED.* Oriental Scholar Presents New and Startling Hypothesis of Creation: Masterpiece of Reasoning.

> And down below:—
> * Genesis, Book of. Dr. Moses. Antioch Press.

Here is a book indeed! Here at last is a solution of the vexed controversy which has divided our scientists for a generation—where Darwinians and Mendelians fall apart in hostile ranks. Dr. Moses, the greatest orientalist, we venture to say, of all times, steps in with a simple, downright solution of the vexed problem of the origin of life. His theory carries with it all the marks of scientific inevitability. We accept it at once frankly and fully as a working hypothesis with the full realization that there are bigger things, simpler things still to come. Simple as Dr. Moses is in this *Book of Genesis*—we understand it is pronounced "Geneesis," deriving from "gen" or "gin" (I am, or should be) "neesis" (not exactly)— we feel that he can be simpler still and that what we have here is only a first *reductio ad absurdum.*

Meantime, even here, the great Oriental scholar cuts his way through every difficulty. Realizing the extent to which the problem of the origin of life was hampered by our imperfect knowledge of physical and chemical science, Dr. Moses takes the bold course of disregarding these altogether. He does not even mention the Newtonian theory of light, and replaces both the Copernican Theory and the Ptolemaic cycle and epicycle by the simple conception of a firmament lighted with lamps.

In regard to the origin of animal life Dr. Moses cuts the Gordian knot of controversy by bringing on the animals two by two. This gets away at once from Darwin's dilemma as to how they came to be different. Dr. Moses shows us that they always were.

The chapters of the book in regard to the Primitive Garden make delightful reading, especially at this time of the year, and garden lovers will find Dr. Moses an interesting and instructive cicerone. We recognized many of our old favorites in his garden, while at the same time Dr. Moses, himself a horticultural enthusiast, introduces us to a number of varieties of edible plants not previously known to our culinary science.

Dr. Moses writes a clear and scholarly style, ending each sentence before beginning the next one, and dividing his sentences with full stops. We hope that this first essay will be followed by others. We would like him to write a book on Exodus and certainly one on Deuteronomy, both of which topics would suit him, we will not say to a T, but to a Dageesh.

THE INVASION OF HUMAN THOUGHT BY MATHEMATICAL SYMBOLS

For Economics, Mathematical Symbolism Is the Means Adopted

I

IT is to be feared that many readers of this book will pass this essay by—the modest as too learned, the learned as too ignorant; the light as too heavy, and the heavy as too light. All will be mistaken. What is here said is very real truth—even if softened now and again with an attempt to alleviate it by what is very real fun—and represents a very real and important issue.

The clergy, in their similar despairing call for attention at the opening of a sermon, take a text. Let me, therefore, as the prelude to this essay, take mine from the pages of one of the most eminent and conspicuous works in economics that has appeared in the past few years. The writer of it is the holder of one of the most respected chairs in England, in a university of which I dare not breathe the name. If I did, I should be crushed flat at once under the dead weight of prestige and authority. In any case it would seem invidious and personal to say that in my opinion the particular book of a particular author is tommyrot, when what I really mean is that a hundred recent books by a hundred recent authors are tommyrot.

The author in the case before us is undertaking a discussion of what he calls the "size of real incomes." That is about as near to a plain intelligible phrase as a trained economist can get. An ordinary person would prefer to say "what people get for their money," but that would be just a little too easy to understand. The writer goes on to say that if, conceivably, all people used and consumed one and the same thing, and only one, then we could compare what each got with what every other got by the mere quantity or number. But in reality people consume all kinds of different things with all kinds of preferences.

So far the sky is clear. There has been no warning of mathematics. The readers are as unsuspecting as the crowd in the Paris streets before Napoleon Bonaparte turned on the grapeshot of Vendémiaire.

Now comes the volley:—

It may perhaps be thought that the difficulty can be overcome by comparing real incomes, not in themselves, but in respect of their values. It is, of course, always possible, with a pricing system, to value each of two real incomes in terms of any commodity that we choose, and to set the values so reached over against one another. This is frequently done in terms of money. Unfortunately, however, the two valuations will, in general, be related to one another in different ways according to what commodity is taken as the measure of value. Thus, suppose that we have two incomes each comprising items of three sorts— A, B, C; that in the first income the quantities of these items are a, b, c, with money prices p_a, p_b, p ; and in the second α, β, γ, with money prices π_a, π_β, π_γ. The money value of the first income divided by that of the second is then $\dfrac{ap_a + bp_b + cp_c}{\alpha\pi_a + \beta\pi_\beta + \gamma\pi_\gamma}$. Call this m. The value of the first income divided by that of the second in terms of commodity A is $\dfrac{\pi_a}{p_a}$ m; in terms of commodity B, $\dfrac{\pi_\beta}{p_b}$ m; in terms of commodity C, $\dfrac{\pi_\gamma}{p_c}$ m. These quantities are obviously, in general, different. There is nothing to prevent one of them being greater, while another is less, than unity. Thus the result of comparisons depends on the choice we make of the commodity in terms of which valuations are to be made; and this is purely arbitrary. Nothing useful, therefore, can be accomplished on this plan.

As the last echo of the paragraph dies away, the readers are seen to lie as thickly mown down as the casualties of Vendémiaire. The volley has done its work. There will be no further resistance to the argument on the part of the general public. Theirs not to reason why, theirs but to do and die. They will learn to surrender their economic thought to the dictation of the élite. They are not to question where they do not understand.

The last sentence of the paragraph, the final shot, is not without humor. "Nothing useful," it says, "can be accomplished on this plan." No, indeed, nothing much, except getting rid of the readers. For the whole of the "plan" and its pretentious mathematics, when interpreted into plain talk, amounts to something so insignificant and so self-evident that it is within reach of the simplest peasant who ever lived in Boeotia, or failed at Cambridge. It only means that different people with the same money would buy different things; one might buy roses, one cigars, and another concert tickets; and you couldn't very well compare them because the weight wouldn't mean anything, and the color wouldn't, nor the number. As to what you pay for them *in money* and why you paid—well, that is the very thing we want to find out.

Or shall I state the same thing like this: "It is hard to compare Janie's doll with Johnny's dog." Or let us put it into rural Yorkshire: "There's a mowt of folks i' counthry; happen one loike this an' t'other chap that; dang me if I know 'oo gets best on it." Or in Cree Indian (Fort Chipewyan, H. B. Post, Athabaska Lake) : "Hole-in-the-Sky take four guns, two blanket; squaw take one looking glass, one hymn-book."

What the problem means is that he can't really compare what Hole-in-the-Sky got and what the squaw got. That's all.

II

What has been just said is not meant as fun: it is meant in earnest. If the mathematical statement helped the thought—either in presentation or in power of deduction—it would be worth while. But it doesn't. It impedes it. It merely helps to turn economics into an esoteric science, known only to the few. The mathematician is beckoning economics toward the seclusion of the dusty chamber of death, in the pyramid of scholasticism. He stands at the door that he has opened, his keys in his hand. It is dark within and silent. In the darkness lie the mummified bodies of the learnings that were, that perished one by one in the dead mephitic air of scholasticism; of learning that had turned to formalism and lost its meaning, to body and lost its soul, to formula and lost its living force. Here lie, centuries old, the

Scholarship of China, the Learning of Heliopolis, the Medicine that the Middle Ages killed, and the Reason that fell asleep as Formal Logic.

All are wrapped in a sanctity that still imposes. They sleep in all the symbols of honor, with a whisper of legend still about them. But the work they would not do, the task they could not fulfill, is left still to the fresh bright ignorance of an inquiring world.

Put without prolixity: Any well-established dignified branch of knowledge, finding its problems still unsolved, turns to formalism, authority, symbolism, the inner system of a set of devotees, excluding the world; philosophy becomes scholasticism, science turns to thaumaturgy, religion to dogma, language rhetoric, and art to symbolism.

Modern economics and philosophy and psychology have so far utterly failed to solve their main problems. So they are beginning to "dig in" as scholasticism. For economics, mathematical symbolism is the means adopted.

III

So few people are accustomed to use mathematical symbols that it is hard to discuss them in an essay of this sort without incurring the very danger here denounced and "sidetracking" the reader. But something of their nature everybody knows. Very often a mathematical symbol or expression does convey an idea very quickly and clearly. Thus the simple and self-evident little charts and graphs used in newspapers to show the rise and fall of production and trade, the elementary index numbers used to show the movement of prices—these things are immensely useful. But they are only a method of presentation of what is known, not a method of finding out what is not known.

Very often we use simple mathematical expressions as a vehicle of common language, as when we say "fifty-fifty," or "a hundred per cent American," or "half-soused," or "three-quarters silly." We could go further if we liked, and instead of saying "more and more" we could say $A + n + n. . . .$ We could express a lot of our ordinary dialogue in mathematical form. Thus:—

"How is your grandmother's health?"
"Oh, it depends a good deal on the weather and her digestion, but I am afraid she always fusses about herself: today she's about fifty-fifty."

Mathematically this is a function of two variables and a constant, and reads:—

$$f(W.D. + fuss) = \tfrac{1}{2}$$

The result is, in all seriousness, just as illuminating and just as valuable as the mathematics quoted above.

We could even go further and express a lot of our best poetry in mathematical form:—

TENNYSON'S "LIGHT BRIGADE"

Half a league, half a league,
   Half a league onward . . .
Then they rode back, but not,
   Not the six hundred.

The mathematician would prefer:—

$$\frac{½ + ½ + ½}{600} = 600 - N$$

Or, try this as an improvement on Byron:—

CHILDE HAROLD'S PILGRIMAGE

Did ye not hear it?—No; 'twas but the wind,
Or the car rattling o'er the stony street;
On with the dance!

$$d + d + d + d \; . \; . \; . \; d \; (n)$$

   Let joy be unconfined;

$$j + j + j + \; . \; . \; . \; infinity$$

No sleep till morn, when Youth and Pleasure meet.

$$M - S = Y + P$$

Or, to quote a verse of "Lord Ullin's Daughter" (done as mathematics), in which I once depicted the desperate efforts of the Highland boatman:—

The angry water gains apace
Both of his sides and half his base,

Till as he sits he seems to lose
The square of his hypotenuse.

Or, to go a little deeper, by venturing into Descartes's brilliant method of indicating space and motion by means of two or more coördinates as a frame of reference, we can make the opening of Gray's "Elegy" a little more exact.

The lowing herd winds slowly o'er the lea.

We can indicate the exact path by a series of points at successive moments of time $(p - p_1 - p_2 - p_3 \ldots p_n)$, and by dropping perpendiculars from each of these to the coördinates we can indicate the area swept by the lowing herd, or rather the area which it ought to sweep but doesn't.

IV

Let me explain here that in this essay I do not wish in any way to deny the marvelous effectiveness of mathematical symbols in their proper field. I have for mathematics that lowly respect and that infinite admiration felt by those of us who never could get beyond such trifles as plane trigonometry and logarithms, and were stopped by a *nolle prosequi* from the penetration of its higher mysteries. Mathematical symbols permit of calculation otherwise beyond our powers and of quantitative expression that otherwise would require an infinity of time. It is no exaggeration to say that mathematical symbols are second only to the alphabet as an instrument of human progress. Think what is entailed by the lack of them. Imagine a Roman trying to multiply LXXVI by CLX. The Roman, indeed, could make use of an abacus—the beads on wires of the Chinese, the familiar nursery toy—but multiplication with beads only, and without written symbols on a decimal or ascending place-plan, is a poor and limited matter. See who will in this connection the mediaeval work called *Accomptyng by Counters*—A.D. 1510.

Contrast with these feeble expedients the power of expression and computation that symbols give us! The Hebrew psalmist used to ask with awe who could number the sands of the sea! Well, I can! Put them, let us say, at $(100)^{100}$ and we've only used six figures and two crooked lines! And if that is not enough use three more figures:—

$$100^{100^{100^{100}}}$$

Where are the sands of the sea now? Gone to mud! Light moves fast and space is large, but symbols can shoot past them at a walk. Take the symbol for a "light-year" and cube it! You can see it all there in half a dozen strokes, and its meaning is as exact as the change out of a dollar.

Consider this. There is a famous old Persian story, known to everybody, of the grateful king who asked the physician who had saved his life to name his own reward. The physician merely asked that a penny— or an obol or something—be placed on the first square of a chessboard, two on the next, and then four, and so on, till all the sixty-four spaces were filled! The shah protested at the man's modesty and said he must at least take a horse as well. Then they counted the money, and presumably the shah fell back dead! The mathematical formula that killed him was the series $(1 + 2 + 4 \ldots N)$, where $N = 64$: the sum of a geometrical progression—and, at that, the simplest and slowest one known to whole numbers.

As a matter of fact, if the king and the physician had started counting out the pennies at the rate of five thousand an hour and had kept it up for a seven-hour day, with Sundays off, it would have taken them a month to count a million. At the end of a year they'd be only on square No. 20 out of the sixty-four; granting that the king and the physician were each sixty-two years old (they'd have to be that to have got so far in politics), their expectation of life would be fifteen years, and they'd both be dead before they got to the thirtieth square; and the last square alone would call for 10,000,000,000,000,000,000 pennies. In other words, they are both alive now and counting.[1] Yet any mathematician, with a table of logarithms and a lead-pencil, would work out their calculation in five minutes.

V

But all of this wonder and power and mystery is of no aid in calculating the incalculable. You cannot express the warmth of emotions in calories, the pressure on the market in horsepower, and the buoyancy of credit in specific gravity! Yet this is exactly what the pseudo-mathematicians try to do when they invade the social sciences. The conceptions dealt with in politics and economics and psychology—the ideas of valuation, preference, willingness and unwillingness, antipathy, desire, and so forth—cannot be put into quantitative terms.

It would not so much matter if this vast and ill-placed mess of mathematical symbolism could be set aside and left to itself while the real work of economics went on. Thus, for example, is left aside by the real modern physicists, such as Rutherford and Soddy, the whole mass of the Einstein geometry—which from their point of view is neither here nor there. (Many people don't know that.) But in the case of economic theory these practitioners undertake to draw deductions; to dive into a cloud of

[1] If any reader doubts these calculations I refer him to my colleague, Professor Charles Sullivan of McGill University, and if he doubts Professor Sullivan I refer him so far that he will never get back.—AUTHOR.

mathematics and come out again holding a theory, a precept, an *order*, as it were, in regard to the why of the depression, or a remedy for unemployment, or an explanation of the nature of saving and investment. They are like—or want to be like—a physician prescribing a dose for the docile and confiding patient. He writes on a piece of paper, "$\sigma\Delta\rho_0^0$," and says, "Take that." Thus one of the latest and otherwise most deservedly famous of the mathematical economists advises us in a new book, heralded as the book of the year, that our salvation lies in the proper adjustment of investment and demand. Once get this right and all the rest is easy. As a first aid the great economist undertakes to explain the relation of investment and demand in a preliminary, simple fashion as follows:—

More generally the proportionate change in total demand to the proportionate change in investment equals

$$\frac{\Delta Y}{Y} \bigg/ \frac{\Delta.I}{I} = \frac{\Delta Y}{Y}.\frac{Y-C}{\Delta Y - \Delta C} = \frac{1 - \dfrac{c}{y}}{1 - \dfrac{dc}{dy}}$$

To 99.9 per cent of the world's readers this spells good-bye. If economics can only be made intelligible in that form, then it moves into the class of atomic physics. The great mass of us are outside of it. We can judge it only by its accomplishments; and, as economics so far has accomplished nothing, the outlook is dark.

Now I do not know what all that Delta and Y stuff just quoted means, but I am certain that if I did I could write it out just as plainly and simply as the wonderful theorem up above about different people spending their money on different things. In other words, mathematical economics is what is called in criminal circles "a racket."

The kind of calculation involved is all right in real mathematics. But on examination, by those able to examine it, it always contains the grossest of fallacies when it tries to measure what can't be measured. The money-economist, for instance, starts a calculation of prices involving such immeasurables as "public confidence" or that good old friend the "velocity of money." Not being able to measure either of these at all, he calls confidence C and velocity V; then they get lost in a cloud of figures, and the error multiplies itself to infinity.

Few people have stopped to consider this statistical fallacy of the multiplication of error—that is, of the kind of error or inexactitude which increases as it goes. If I use a pair of compasses to measure a diagram on a bit of paper, a shift in the opening angle of one degree is nothing at all. But if I use it to project it into space—"to sweep an area" as the physicists and the housemaids say—then the error runs to a universe.

.   .   .   .

In ancient history the Parthians, without hope of overcoming the organized Roman Legion, would turn in their flight and shoot a departing arrow on a chance errand. Such a "Parthian shaft" may be here essayed in conclusion. Reading as best I could Colonel Arthur Lynch's brilliant book on *The Case Against Einstein,* I am led to suspect that the vast and pretentious structure of the Einstein theory of the Universe is just another case of a vast mathematical "racket."

.   .   .   .

ADDENDUM

After I had written this essay I came across a United States Department of Agriculture Bulletin of the year 1926, which made me realize over again that a government document can interpret an idea far better than private effort.

The bulletin is for the use of Farmers.

Its aim is to reduce the problem of the price of hogs to a definite mathematical forecast. It does so in the following words of hope and encouragement:

As soon as the pig survey has been in operation for a period of time long enough to get a satisfactory measure of the market's response to this new factor it should again be possible to make a highly accurate forecast of hog prices on a mathematical basis.

The bulletin then explains that the method of forecasting will be in the form of a regression equation as follows:

(I) $\log_{11} X = -0.09443 \log X_1, +0.15888 \log X_2 - 0.21986 \log X_3 - 0.23675 \log X_4 - 0.07250 \log X_5 + 2.23777 \log X_6 + 0.04759 \log X_7 + 0.22659 \log X_8 - 0.03036 X_9 + 1.63099 \log X_{10} - K.$

When the hogs hear this, it's all up with them.

IMAGINARY PERSONS

From John Doe to John Bull: From Punch and Judy to Brother Jonathan

IT is characteristic of mankind that our dreams are better than our waking hours, our fiction than our daily lives and our imagination superior to reality. This arises, shall we say, from the existence within each of us of a sort of imprisoned super-self, conscious of a better world than the one about us. Only in our higher moments—in the thrill of danger, in the flush of creative effort, in the benevolence of Christmas—do we enter for a brief space within it. But we carry round, in much that we do and say, certain vestiges of this better world, like the poet's trailing clouds of glory.

Nor is there any better instance of this than in our intercourse with the queer set of imaginary persons whom we have created out of next to nothing to be the companions of our pilgrimage. I am not thinking here of the characters of fiction, the people "out of a book." Such people as Huckleberry Finn and Mr. Pickwick and Sherlock Holmes belong elsewhere. The people I mean were never in a book, or if they were, escaped from it so long ago and so completely that all trace of their origin was lost, and they entered upon a life of their own. I am thinking, in other words, of such persons as Davy Jones, and Jack Robinson, of Punch and Judy, John Doe and Richard Roe, and John Bull and Uncle Sam. All these are real enough and all carry with them the queer imprint of super-self in belonging to a better world than that of our daily walk.

Of many of them the origin is utterly lost; of others it can be traced back a certain distance and then disappears; of others, again, it is quite traceable as a matter of scholarship, but quite unknown to those who daily deal with its descendant. Who, for example, was Jack Robinson? Except for the fact that his name became a symbol for rapid speech, and that things happen before we can say Jack Robinson, we know nothing of the man. He apparently has a French cousin called Jean de Nivelle, known not for his own sake but for his dog—"*qui s'enfuie quand on l'appelle*." But that is all we know of him, unless he is one of the trio "Brown, Jones and Robinson," otherwise familiarly known as "Tom, Dick and Harry."

But look at Punch and Judy whose origin we know absolutely. What a grim tragedy of human history is reflected here! This queer jocular Punch who fights with Judy in his little show-box, wicked without knowing it, all agrin with malice, that seems somehow to run the gamut of emotion and turn to merriment! Who is this? This is—save the mark!—Pontius Pilate, come down from a sacred miracle play of the Middle Ages, and the Judy with him is Judas Iscariot. What a commentary on the story of mankind, in which the most tragic chapter of human history is turned to the laughter of country clowns! It is like the "*hoc est corpus*" of the sacrament which slowly passed into "*hocus pocus.*" Yet the real significance of Punch is that in the course of time even the greatest of our sorrows takes on the soft colouring of retrospect, that in the long run human happiness wins out over human suffering. It must be so or our lot would be too hard to bear. We are compelled as it were to "laugh it off."

Oddly enough Punch and Judy, as they passed down the decades of history, picked up other accessory characters not part of the original miracle play. The baby which they throw about originated in the change of Judy's sex from that of Judaeus, though it may have an irreverent origin of its own. The dog "Toby" seems straight out of the infernal pit; he may be Tobias, son of Tobit of the Apocrypha. Another character who came into the Punch story much later is Jack Ketch, a sort of imaginary or generalized hangman. The English Punch and Judy picture books put him in on the last page, carrying his portable gibbet, with the legend, "In the end Jack Ketch comes to hang Punch." His face is concealed after the correct fashion of the executioners of his time. As a matter of fact Jack Ketch once existed as the "headsman" of King Charles II and King James II's reign. Apparently he was a very poor one. Macaulay tells of his beheading the unhappy Duke of Monmouth on Tower Hill in 1685. "Monmouth," he writes, "accosted John Ketch, the executioner, a wretch who had already butchered many brave and noble victims, and whose name during a century and a half has been vulgarly given to all those who have succeeded him in his odious office. 'Here,' said the Duke, 'are six guineas for you. Do not hack me as you did my Lord Russell.' " After which Macaulay describes the hideous scene of butchery that followed as Ketch hacked away with blow after blow at his wretched victim.

Out of all this has come our Mr. Punch, chastened somehow of all wickedness, a genial character whom we know as well as ourselves—"as pleased as Punch," we say, or "as proud as Punch," using him as what the mathematicians called a "frame of reference."

Punch thus represents a full and elaborate record. Other imaginary people are often connected only with a single attribute or a single performance. Thus Davy Jones has no other function except to keep a "locker" to which drowned sailors go. His name is really "Duffy" Jones—"duffy" being a Negro word for ghost. He is the ghost of Jones, that is to say of Jonah of the Old Testament whose nautical experiences are well known. His pious origin is paralleled in the nautical sphere by that of Mother Carey (Mater Cara) whose chickens are the storm-petrels. Very different is "Mother Goose" of the nursery rhymes who was actually a Mrs. Goose and kept a little shop and sold nursery books in bygone Boston. But who is Gilroy who had the kite? People of fairly ripe age will recall how frequently, about fifty years ago, we used to talk of things being "knocked as high as Gilroy's Kite." I never heard of anyone investigating who Gilroy was. But I think I can guess it—or as Sherlock Holmes would say "deduce" it. When the first suspension bridge was to be built over the Niagara Gorge, a prize was offered for the first kite to be successfully flown to carry a string across. Something tells me that must have been Gilroy's kite.

But the two prize winners among imaginary people are the famous characters John Doe and Richard Roe. I defy anyone to find out their origin. It is easy enough to trace them back for five or six hundred years. That's nothing. But what were they before that? They grew to maturity—or rather like Pallas they leap into full size—in the law courts of the Middle Ages. They appear as imaginary people used as legal fictions to appear where real people could not be cited. This was chiefly in the case of claims against owners of land. The Middle Ages—and indeed England until quite modern times—had a great regard for the sanctity of property in land. To disturb it was "taboo." In an age before scientific record and documentation, *possession* was everything—"nine points of the law," as the old phrase had it. Hence the common law courts in England could not directly entertain suits for ejecting a man in actual possession. What was done was this. The claimant to the land conveyed all his rights to his good friend John Doe. In early times he was not restricted to John Doe: there was a rival person called, rather transparently, "Thomas Goodtitle." But he was offensively obvious and dropped out. John Doe, as soon as he got his communication (which is reality he never got, but the law acted for him), then got out a writ against a man called Richard Roe on the ground that Roe was keeping him by force out of his property. Here again there was a mediaeval alternative in "William Styles of Newbury in the County of Berks," but Heaven knows how he ever got in and he proved too explicit to survive. Hence John Doe and Richard Roe got the whole field and kept it for centuries. The writ that Doe swore out against Roe accused him of terrible things, namely that he had "with force of arms, that is to say, with swords and staves and knives entered into the said tenement with the appurtenances and ejected the said John out of his said tenement and other wrongs him did." This bloodthirsty accusation passed harmless off Richard Roe's accustomed hide. He answered, without heat, that, while he himself had no concern with the property, he was aware that such and such a person (naming the man in possession) was actually sitting on it and suggested calling him into court to say what he knew. This did the trick and the suit for ejectment went right ahead without needing John and Richard. In any case they had other things to do. They were always busy, having picked up a variety of odd functions. For example, they supplied bail for debtors, etc. The old law did not allow a man to put up money to bail himself, but John Doe could put it up for him; so he gave it to John Doe first. This "common bail" naturally proved very often ineffective and led to the demand for "special bail" which Doe couldn't give, having no special existence.

Poor Doe and Roe came to an end as far as England is concerned with the sweeping law reforms of 1852. Ejectment suits were made by a direct process, their other uses were terminated and Doe and Roe expired by act of parliament. The lawyers of the London Inn's, who had made a harvest from them for centuries, celebrated their demise with banquets, toasts and witty memorial verses. One such runs:—

Now Doe and Roe 'tis grief to tell
For law's reform you die,
And as I bid you both farewell
A tear bedims my eye—

and on which follows an "Old lang syne" chorus.

Doe and Roe however survive in the United States, where they keep still one of their earlier English activities. Their names are used in the pursuit of criminals whom they are supposed to have assisted. Thus in trying to arrest the imaginary John Doe, the law apprehends the real criminal—or fails to.

Equally conspicuous among imaginary people are those who stand for a whole nation at a time, such as, most triumphantly, John Bull and Uncle Sam. No other two nations have so successfully embodied themselves in abstraction as have the British and the American. Beside these heroes, such creations as John Chinaman, Fritz, etc., are hopelessly vague, and others like Jack Canuck feeble and ineffective. But John Bull and Uncle Sam actually live and breathe. Oddly enough "John Bull" originally came out of an eighteenth-century book, long forgotten. He stepped so far out of it, and the book was forgotten so completely, that his existence has nothing further to do with it. We see the same thing happening today to Sherlock Holmes, who has been "generalized" far beyond his creator's pages. People in dis-

tant countries talk of him who never read a word
of him. So with John Bull; he has from the eighteenth
century his appetite, his rolled-top boots, his costume
of a country squire in a market town, and with
that he carries forward from generation to generation.

Uncle Sam had a more complicated origin. His
actual name was taken out of the letters U. S., which
arose with the independence of the United States;
the anagram, or joke, or whatever you call it must
have occurred not to any one person only, as often
narrated, but to hundreds. It is so obvious. But the
character was not properly created till the "Comic
Yankee" had been worked out on the stage (where
Uncle Sam got his clothes) and exploited by Major
Jack Downing and such chroniclers.

Once created, Uncle Sam went strong. But as a
matter of fact he had for many years a sort of rival,
or alternate, in the form of "Brother Jonathan."
This was the same character, more or less, but without the full habiliment. Jonathan was a real person,
a certain Jonathan Turnbull of Revolutionary times,
on whom George Washington greatly relied. The
nickname "Brother Jonathan" is right out of history, the words being Washington's. But Uncle Sam
proved the better type—and survived. A recent
entertaining writer has told us that Uncle Sam
exactly represents the American face and physique

of the pioneering days, the "roaring forties." The days of the Revolution, he says, tended to produce the statesmanlike faces of lawyers and politicians: the pioneer days the rough energetic faces of Abraham Lincoln and Uncle Sam; the modern days of city life and office existence produce a face much like an apple. Leaving out of question the apple theory—which no foreigner would dare to endorse—the Uncle Sam part of the idea certainly sounds good.

One realizes better the actuality of Uncle Sam and John Bull when we turn to countries like Canada which have no such national personification. Our papers use at times a draped female, always either suspiciously stout or distressingly thin, or else a decidedly vulgar young man in a sort of farm khaki called Jack Canuck, or an old country man, called Ole Man Canada, obviously verging on idiocy.

ADVENTURES IN TORTS

How to Make Laughter Out of Dust

EXTREMES meet. You wouldn't think that Law Books and Tabloid Stories have much in common. But open any book on what the lawyers call Torts or Delicts, or Quasi-Offenses, and you will find that the book is really a collection of fascinating little short stories. The fascination is all the greater from the fact that the law book always leaves out the very thing that the writer of romance is anxious to put in. There is no color, no weather—unless it causes damage—and no human emotions whatever; no love, no hate, just the actions as they come and go.

More than that, the law book never tells the end of the matter—never says what happens next. It gets to the point where someone assessed damages, or didn't, and ends up at that, even if it is obviously leaving family life suspended over a chasm.

I spent a happy afternoon the other day with such a book, a bright little galaxy of fun and fancy entitled *Delicts under the Civil Code of Quebec.*

Here is a sample:—

"A dog, which was owned by A, barked at a horse and caused it to run away and throw its rider, B. It was held that A was liable for the damages sustained by B."

Yes, but how badly was B hurt? It doesn't say. Did he break his back, or was he just what you would call shaken up? And what about the dog? Did A have it shot, or was he fond of it? And are A and B still on speaking terms, or did this incident terminate a friendship of long years?

Not a word said about all that. What might have been a thrilling romance of one hundred pages, thrown away in a few lines.

Here's another:—

"In the waiting room of a railway station, X opened a door with no sign on it, fell downstairs and was killed."

Think of it! But is the law book horrified? Not at all. It seems to think it was a good joke on X. It says:—

"Having indicated the doors for public use, the railway was not negligent when it failed to put notices on doors not intended for public use. The sole effective cause of the accident was the defendant's own want of caution in proceeding beyond the door in the dark in a strange place."

Think how much a romance writer could have made of that: poor X—no doubt under the strain of some great anxiety—groping his way in the dark only to fall headlong! And then what! Who found X after he fell? Did he look pretty awful? Was he killed outright?

But no—the law book is not concerned with that. It merely says: "The railway company was exonerated."

Here is another that I can hardly bear to read:—

"A boy was a trespasser on a roof and as a result . . ."

But no, don't let's read it. The poor little fellow! Fell off the edge or something, I suppose. . . . But the book, I see, does not give the ultimate fate of the boy after he fell. It just says, "Trespassers have no right to complain of the condition of the premises as they find them."

Here's a story with more action in it:—

"A young man, X, employed by a bank which had obtained good references as to his character . . ."

This, you observe, is one of the rare stories with a touch of local color, and very likely the boy X was a son of poor X who was killed in the railway station, and so he got his job out of sympathy for himself and his mother. Anyway, let's see what happened to him:—

"X was required to carry a revolver while accompanying the messenger to the clearing house. Disobeying instructions to replace the revolver in the vault on his return, X, without the knowledge and permission of the bank, kept it in his possession and during the evening shot a boy . . ."

Very likely the poor boy who fell off the roof; shot him as he fell, no doubt.

Here would be the opening of a first-class mystery story. But the law book gets it all hushed up in a few sentences.

"The bank," it says, "was exonerated from liability because, at the time of the shooting, X was not in its employ, nor doing its work."

That's right, too, when you think of it. The bank didn't hire X to go boy-shooting. In fact, as the court put it, *"non fit injuria"*—which means there was no harm done. No, just another boy gone, that's all.

But if you want an afternoon's reading of plots, scenes, and mysteries, enough in one page for a volume, just ask any lawyer to lend you a book on Torts, Delicts, or Quasi-Offenses.

WORDS AND HOW TO USE THEM

A Wise-Crack Above the Beans of Most Guys

THERE has been lately a lot of discussion—renewed discussion—about words and pronunciation. The invention of broadcasting suddenly revealed to us how we all speak, and how differently. The late King George was reported to have dropped an "h" in a broadcast, and millions of hands reached out to pick it up for him. Other hands and voices were raised to deny that he ever dropped it. Thoughtful people wondered what is an "h" anyway? When a Frenchman thinks he puts an "h" in his own word *"hibou"* or in our word "horse," what is he really pronouncing and can you hear it? Out of all which there threatens already to emerge a universal pronunciation, all done like broadcasting. Little children will "broadcast" at breakfast, *"Ma ma may-I-have-an-other-help-ing of po-ridge."*

With that of course goes the question of spelling, with such bright thoughts as "Who put the *b* in debt" and why keep the *p* and the *l* in "psalm" and what use is the letter "c"?

And after that comes the discussion of the words and phrases themselves and the thing called "grammar" which frames them together. Mr. A. P. Herbert's delightful book on *The Word War* came just at the right time to fan the flame. Now that it is dying down again a little there is no harm in poking up the ashes.

.   .   .   .

Personally I am outside of this discussion. I always feel that any expression that I use is *correct*—because I use it—and that when I "enounce" it or pronounce it that settles it. No doubt you feel the same way yourself. No doubt, too, like me, you allow a good deal of latitude. Personally when I see the word *schedule* I am willing to pronounce it—skeddle or skeedle, or skoodle—it's all one. And there are words I keep away from and never say because I can't— such as *pariah,* and *derring-do, banal*—and places I take care not to go to, such as *Przemysl* and *Gdynia* and *Caen.*

But even with the help of indifference it is hard to keep clean outside of the discussion. For example, what are we to think of the new words, or new uses of old ones that are always coming in? Have I the right to call a man a *"lobster"*—even if I admit that he is one? If I see—to use the older form of language—a gentleman taking an outing with two young females, may I describe it as a *"lobster out on a hurrah with a couple of skirts"*? You must remember I've got to call him something. If I can't say a *"lobster"* I'll have to call him a *guy* or a *sport* or a *stiff*—anything except a *gentleman*. That name is kept for hotels, and *individuals* for a police court. As to the women with him, if I don't call them *skirts*, what are they—*Janes, dames*—? certainly not *women*; and *ladies* is almost an insult.

It seems to be a principle of language that all our words wear out with use, as far as point and emphasis are concerned, and become utterly colourless, fit only for a law book. So we have to use new ones that set up some sort of comparison and thereby freshen up the meaning. *Lobster* is only one of the countless ways in which man compares himself to the animals. Doubtful and perplexed as to what he and his fellow men really are, he gets on surer ground if he calls his friend a *lion*, his political leader *battle horse*, and his enemy a *pup*. But all the animals in the front rank got used up long ago. In Shakespeare's plays Antonio called Shylock a *dog*, and Romeo said Juliet was a *duck*. So we have to come down to a lower range and use fish and bugs and things beneath the notice of the classics. When we want to use a term of praise we call a man a *lion*, or perhaps a *tiger*; if we want admiration running a little to good-natured raillery we call him a *whale*. *Dog* works both ways; a man is said to have doglike fidelity, but he is also said to act like a pup. But when we want to get genuine contempt and condemnation, we turn to the fish class and call a man a *lobster* or a *shark* or, most cruel, a *sardine*. One can feel in that word the power and justification of the metaphor. There is something hopeless, humble and inefficient about a sardine. For all its tin box and its oil, it isn't even alive. There are lots of people like that. The man who first called his fellow man a *sardine* was a man of imagination, a poet. Presently it will wear out; a sardine will merely mean a young man of good family who has been to one of the larger colleges.

The case of the birds is peculiar. Their names divide up into compliments, love terms, and terms of scorn, without much rhyme or reason to it. Juliet was a *duck*—so are most girls at eighteen. But why? Watch a duck waddle in and out of a duck pond, flop-footed, quacking, dull-witted—what a thing to be! We can understand our use of *goose* and *hen*—as terms of scorn—but why do we say that a person is a regular *cuckoo?* But the general term *bird* stands as an object of praise and envy from a biped that can't fly.

You see, all these new words are metaphors. So were the old ones. The man who first looked up at the jagged sky line of the mountains of Spain and called them *Sierras* said something. The word means *saws* and it sharpens up one's vision of the mountain. Similarly a "flood" of tears once meant something; a "dilapidated" house was one that fell stone by stone: and a "disaster" came from an unlucky star.

If we didn't allow for the introduction of these new terms our language would soon seem as dull and dead as Egyptian hieroglyphics.

Similarly there is no sense in making ourselves slaves to a set of rules called grammar. For grammar, on final analysis, is only a statement of what we actually say, not of what we *ought to* say. The moment we take to saying something else, then grammar must come along with us. Thus, what is the use of saying, as the grammar book does, "the nominative case must be used after the verb *to be*"? As for instance, "It is I"; "I am he"; "Who is there?" "I." As a matter of fact ninety-nine people (I am one of them) out of a hundred both in America and in England, always say, "It's me." "Who is there?" "Me." The rule won't stand. Consider such a dialogue as this: "Have you seen my gloves anywhere?" "Are these they?" "Oh, thank you, those are they."

The French got over this particular kind of silliness generations ago and always say, "It is *me*," etc. In fact in French the opposite usage, our *good* usage, sounds funny. Do you remember in that witty play *"Ici On Parle Français,"* where someone enters the shop thus indicated as a place where French is spoken and asks:

"Qui est la personne ici qui parle français?"

And the young man behind the counter bows deeply and says, *"Je!"*

That's funny in French, but an English grammarian would fall on the young man's neck and kiss him.

·   ·   ·   ·   ·   ·   ·

We have to remember that the harm done by casual change is much less than the people called "purists" think. A lot of expressions come floating in and out of our language and leave no trace—such things as *"I'll tell the world!"* and *"I'll say so!"* and *"Oh, yeah!"* and *"So's your old man."* They are quickly forgotten. We can hardly remember now that a few years ago *"twenty-three"* suddenly became a sort of catch-word, repeated on every possible occasion. Who can recall now what it stood for? The truth is that to say a thing over and over again, on the principle of repetition for emphasis, is one of the oldest bases of human thought. We don't say a big house, we say a big, big house if we want to make it really large. We say we have come a *long long* way and are *very, very* hungry and so on. Slow-witted people in the country go so far as to tell any good story twice over. They end it and then they turn back and give the final point again—" 'Yes, sir,' he says, says he," and you have to listen again and try to laugh again.

Repetition often carries with it a sort of rhythm which appeals as a matter of sound, quite apart from the sense. I remember how much struck I was with

the wonderful opening lines of one of Mr. A. A.
Milne's nonsensical poems, although as yet I had not
heard any more of it but that. No doubt other people
recall it similarly. It ran: "James James Morison
Morison Wetherby George Debree" . . . So with
the *"I'll say so's"* and the *"Skidoos"* and the *"Twenty-
threes."* We can't keep on making up brilliant things
to say; it would be tiresome anyway; it's better to
repeat.

And so it comes that a lot of words and expressions rise and pass and go. Here and there a real one
—one of inherent force—stays in the language. But
even then it grows stale and worn, loses its point, and
calls for newer expressions to replace it. All our well-
worn combinations, such as a *"hair-breadth escape,"*
"bathed in tears," etc., were once as bright and fresh
as the colours of the morning.

The truth is we have to be tolerant of language.
It is an organic changing thing. But each one of us,
I imagine, draws the line, just as I do, at certain
forms and phrases once and for all not tolerable.
Only everybody's list is different. Certain things I
refuse. For instance I would like to know who
started dragging into the language a lot of new unnecessary verbs, lifted out of the sciences, and supposed to convey great accuracy of physical meaning.
I am thinking of verbs like *"react"* and *"contact"*
and so on. *"React"* is the worst. When I was young

nothing *reacted*—except a pill dissolved in water, or a skittish horse. Now everybody "*reacts*," and has a "*reaction*" to everything. An audience "*reacts*," listeners "*react*," the whole public "*reacts*" and individuals *react* on any provocation. If I go into a bank to borrow fifty dollars I have to consider how the banker will *react*. Perhaps the teller may *react* first, or the janitor as I go out. If in these days you tell a girl that you love her you've got to think of her father's *reaction*. In earlier times he might kick you down the steps but he didn't *react*. And after his reaction you have got to *contact* her mother and after that to *service* the family—a new word that comes in drenched with gasoline to take the place of oblige.

Silliest of all is the language of fiction, especially the language of lovers as represented by their dialogues in up-to-date stories. Lovers are supposed to be so throbbing with passion that ordinary nouns and verbs, especially verbs, don't throb fast enough for them. They have to be speeded up.

Imagine a typical scene of two impassioned lovers parting forever, that is to say, till tomorrow evening.

"Does it have to be?" he gasped.

She shrugged. (Notice not "shrugged her shoulder," presumably more than that, she shrugged from the hips up.)

"You've done it," she threw at him.

"I didn't," he threw back and hit her in the stomach.

"At any rate it's over," she squirted.

"No, no," he yelped.

"Yes," she barked.

He sank down and grassed. All the man was out of him.

. . . .

In conclusion I can only repeat what I said at starting, that for me what I say is right, and the way I say it is correct. And you had better adopt that point of view too. Life changes and you can't stop it anyway by shouting at it. Slang, and free verse, and purists and innovators and renovators, and upholsterers and prudists and nudists come and go and you can't stop them.

MYTHICAL MEN

And What They Are Really Like

MORE and more I realize, as I read the daily papers, that there are living and breathing among us a queer sort of people who may be called MYTHICAL MEN. Everyone knows about them, and yet no one knows them. They are everywhere and nowhere. First and foremost, of course, is the person called—

THE MAN ON THE STREET

It is the peculiarity of this poor creature, apparently, to be wrong about everything. Thus the newspapers say "the man on the street has an erroneous idea," etc., etc. Of course he has. All his ideas are erroneous. Another familiar formula runs "if one were to ask the man on the street for the real reason for such and such a thing—say the chronic troubles in the East—he would probably be at a loss to reply." Of course he would, the poor nut. We can also bet that if he *did* reply his answer would be all wrong. That's what his name is kept in the papers for—just to give wrong answers. Now and again he is allowed to be right but merely to illustrate what a simple matter the question is. Thus it is said "even the man on the street knows that money is not everything," or "even the man on the street is aware that two and two make four."

My mental picture of this poor "man on the street" is as that of a person perpetually being buttonholed and asked questions. He can't walk more than a few yards without someone stopping him and asking him a question, to which he does not know the answer. "If one were to stop the man on the street—" That's the way it always runs. If I were the man on the street, I'd buy a Baby Austin car and sit in behind the curtains and fool them.

Sometimes I suspect that there is more than one man on the street. At times the papers propose to stop, not the man on the street, but "the first man on the street." This implies at least that there is a second man sneaking along behind him. Yet they never talk of stopping the second man; The first one evidently has enough ignorance and simplicity for both of them.

Think how simple he is! The "man on the street" always expects spring two weeks before it comes; had no notion that China and Japan were going to war; never guesses right as to who will be the Democratic candidate; thinks the French a warlike nation; little realizes—oh, there is no end to what he doesn't little realize.

Now contrast him with that other mythical person

who appears almost as frequently in the press under the name of—

THE WELL-INFORMED MAN

Ah, now, here's a real fellow. For example, the well-informed man knows that the total Mohammedan population of the globe largely outnumbers the Christian. You see, that's just the kind of thing he *does* know. Now the man on the street would confuse the Mohammedans with the niggers and be all out in his estimate. But the well-informed man hits it every time. He knows that there are no trees in Iceland (of course not); that the diameter of the earth is 7916 miles (he couldn't miss it); that the Treaty of Versailles was not signed by the Republic of Latvia; and that sea water freezes at a lower temperature than soda water.

THE REASONABLE MAN

Another of these mythical figures, almost as much to be admired as the well-informed man, is the individual known as the Reasonable Man. This person, in the eye of the law, actually exists. He is used in the settlement of law suits, family quarrels, valuation of damages, and such things. The especial point about the Reasonable Man is that he is never moved by emotion, never touched by love, never heated by anger, never affected by favouritism. He's just "reasonable." He will divide up an acre of land with you half and half, take his proper share of an inheritance and no more, and do what a traffic officer tells him to. The "Reasonable Man" of the law ought to be more widely known and used. He would really be invaluable in daily life—for instance, in dividing up the last two drinks in a bottle, or deciding whether a bobtail straight beats a four-card flush.

THE WELL-DRESSED MAN

Sitting beside any of these, but not talking, because he never speaks, is the figure of the *Well-dressed Man*, whose wishes, desires and insistencies form a large feature in up-to-date advertising. As he sits he adjusts his leg so as to show the gloss of his boot and the fold of his trousers. He has an absolutely brand-new hat (he never uses anything more than one day), which he holds in his hand in order to give point to his statement that this spring he "insists upon grey." If we could see through his clothes, we would see that he has suspenders with little wheels because he "refuses to wear any others"; also his socks come up and down with little pulleys; indeed there is running gear all over him. But he never speaks. He can't. They took his entire brain out by a surgical operation when he qualified for the part of the *Well-dressed Man*.

THE AVERAGE MAN

The little group can be completed by the addition of the person called the *Average Man*. This individual we know to a nicety. He is five feet nine inches tall, thirty-eight inches round the chest, and lives for fifty-eight years during which time he has two and a half children. In fact, everything he does can be, and has been, calculated to a hair.

.   .   .   .

I have often thought that it would be interesting to get this little group of mythical people together. What, for instance, would happen if one could meet this little crowd and ask each of them one and the same question, and see how they would answer it. Suppose, for example, we had them all together, let us say in the lobby of a hotel, or the lounge room of a club (by the way, the "man in the street" wouldn't know the difference) and asked of each of them, "When do you think the present depression will be over?"

The *Average Man* answers at once: "You can search me. I don't know." *The Man in the Street* replies, "Last year I kept thinking it would end sooner than I thought it would, but I don't think it."

The *Reasonable Man* says, "There seems every reason to think that as soon as it has run its course it must come to a finish, so that the end ought to be in sight pretty soon after we get past the last stages of it."

The *Well-informed Man* answers that the sharp rise in Belgian steel would indicate that the whole thing is over, if it weren't that the fall in the price of hay in Finland may affect the market for eggs in Czecho-Slovakia.

The *Well-dressed Man* smiles and says nothing. He hadn't known there had been any depression.

So in the end, all the five Mythical Men seem much the same man after all.

INTERVIEWS AS THEY WERE AND ARE

(The Interview with a Famous Actress as Done in 1896)

MADAME STODGESKA, the famous actress now opening her American Shakespearian tour, gave an interview to a representative of *The Home and Fireside* in her suite at the George Washington Hotel. Madame Stodgeska stated that when she left England the health of Queen Victoria was excellent. She stated that she had always wanted to see the United States and now she saw it. She thought she could best describe it as a country with a future. Madame Stodgeska said that she was delighted to have the opportunity of playing in Shakespeare. "After all," she said, "who has ever equalled Shakespeare?"

(Here the reporter fell asleep.)

.   .   .   .   .   .

(Interview with a Movie Queen of 1936)

[Specially fabricated by Mr. Ritemore Trasche.

Scoop!!! Revealed for the first time!
The hidden LOVE-LIFE of Miss Eloise De La Chic!!]

.   .   .   .   .   .

"The only reason that I ever became great," announced Miss De La Chic, sitting curvaciously but precariously on the edge of her chair and smoking a fifty-cent Habana cigar, "is that in early life I was crossed in love, and was thus enabled to explore to its depths my misunderstood soul."

"Oh, my, my! isn't that just too divine! Do tell, Miss De La Chic," I gurgled.

"I intend to," she answered, blowing some cigar smoke into my face. "Now that I am a success in the motion pictures, I feel that I may tell what was once the darkest secret of my life, a secret which I vowed my ruby lips (I use Sheik's Dream, model 34, lipstick, one dollar a jar, which is guaranteed to turn you in one night from a wallflower into the most sought-after woman in the room, write for a free sample) should never disclose. In my youth I was deeply and passionately in love with the gentleman who used to bring us our letters, the postman. With every living fibre of my girlish soul I worshipped that man. In the daytime, while at work, I would sit for long hours, gazing moodily through the adding-machine, dreaming . . . dreaming that some day he and I might perhaps have a home of our own . . . a little gray cottage surrounded by roses, and spaghetti, and . . . and everything like that. One day I even forgot myself so far as to bite my employer's ear as I sat on his knee, taking dictation. At night while I was . . . ah, sewing with Mother, I would often catch myself darning the legs of father's Sunday pants together, before I would realize that I was thinking of someone nearer and dearer to me than life itself.

"Ah, me! Shakespeare once said when he was lecturing in Des Moines, Iowa. 'If you don't know what's what, you're a darn sight better off for not knowing it.' I can appreciate the full meaning of that statement now. For quite a time my life of bliss and adoration went on, and my love for the postman deepened as day succeeded day.

"Then one morning he brought his kids with him as he delivered the mail. Seven dirty little boys and eight filthy little girls; I counted them twice to make sure. The cad! Oh, the unspeakable cad! I could have choked him on the spot! As it was, the shock nearly killed me. For years I lay hovering between life and death, able only to exist on Caviar, Cliquot '93 and lobster salad à la Conchini. Mother suggested a breach of promise case, but my better feelings prevailed over her and I told her that never, never could I bring myself to sue the man I had once loved so dearly; besides, I had lost his letters and the lock of hair he gave me.

"When I recovered I was completely changed. From an innocent and beautiful young gazelle, I had turned into a beautiful and hardened, yet charmingly sophisticated, woman of the world—as I am today. From then on I devoted myself to the stage and screen, and quickly developed great poise and charm in my acting, and not only that but tremendous dramatic poignancy and exactness of character . . . and, of course, I had my beauty.

"Still, although I have reached the top rung of the ladder of success, I may say that basically I have not changed. My heart is that of a schoolgirl, of a poor schoolgirl who gave her trusting heart to one whose perfidity was so vile as to be unspeakable.

"And now, Mr. Trasche, if you'll excuse me I have to go and make up for the title rôle in the film *Lady of Modesty*. I am the star, of course."

WHAT HAPPENED NEXT?

The Sequel to Some Famous World Stories

I THINK it was Mark Twain who once explained that most of the famous anecdotes and stories stopped too soon and ought to have been carried on to show what happened next. It was either Mark Twain or Artemus Ward or somebody. At any rate, the idea is a good one.

Here, for example, to begin on, are one or two very familiar applications of it to the famous stories of the ancient world.

ANDROCLES AND THE LION

"A poor Christian Nubian, named Androcles, once found a sick lion in the jungle with a great thorn in its foot. Moved by compassion Androcles removed the thorn, tended the lion, and restored it to health. Later on the two again met. This time it was in the arena at Rome at a great gladiatorial spectacle. The lion had been captured in the jungle and sent to Rome, and Androcles, himself also captured into slavery, was thrown into the arena to be devoured by the lion. But to the surprise of the vast populace which crowded the arena, the lion, instead of leaping upon Androcles to devour him, came up to him and licked his hands and feet with evident affection."

Sequel.

"There followed a few moments of painful surprise and disappointment. After which Quintus Marcus Valerius, the ringmaster, called out, 'Oh, Bill, fetch another lion.' "

.   .   .   .

and to the same effect:—

ARCHIMEDES AND HIS "EUREKA"

"One day Archimedes, the famous Greek mathematician of ancient Syracuse, was sitting in his bath (or more likely he was lying) and was thinking of a profound problem in mathematical physics. He wished to find some way to test whether a crown supposed to be made only of pure gold did or did not contain alloy. And he wanted to find it out without melting or defacing the crown. All of a sudden the solution of the problem occurred to him, and the philosopher in great excitement leaped from his bath and rushed down the street, shouting out 'Heureka! Heureka!—I have found it!' "

Such is the story. But to make it complete, the sequel should be added, thus:

"The ancient world, however, had its own notions of propriety and public decency. Archimedes was immediately arrested by the police of Syracuse, and heavily fined for wearing a towel in public."

. . . .

There is another type of famous anecdote in which the story needs not so much completion as correction. It has evidently got tangled up by telling and retelling till its original form is altogether lost. But we are able, by applying parallel experiences of the present day, to put it back to what it was, thus:

WILLIAM TELL AND THE APPLE

"In the days of the Austrian tyranny over the cantons of Switzerland there lived a brave patriot named William Tell. Tell was brought before the cruel Governor Gesler on suspicion that he was conspiring to revolt. 'Tell,' said the Austrian, 'I hear that you are said to be the best shot with the crossbow in all the cantons. Prove it by shooting an apple off your son's head, and I will let you go free.' The little Tell was placed in position and stood calmly with the apple on his head. Tell (Senior) took aim and his arrow cleft the apple in two. Gesler noticed a second arrow in Tell's belt. 'What need of the second arrow,' he said, 'if you had killed your son with the first?' 'The second arrow was for you,' replied Tell. The meeting broke up with expressions of mutual esteem."

. . . .

Now, really, does that sound likely? A governor
let off a revolutionist merely because he could hit an
apple! They don't do it. The truth is that the whole
story has got badly garbled in the lapse of centuries.
In fact, from what we know now we can easily reconstruct the real scene.

.　　　.　　　.　　　.　　　.　　　.　　　.

" 'What ever are we to do,' said Governor Gesler
to his secretary, 'about these freak exhibitions of
skill? The thing is getting dangerous. It must be
stopped.'

"Just then a messenger appeared at the door.

" 'There's a Swiss gentleman outside who says he
has something to show to your Excellency.'

"Gesler, always anxious to please his subjects,
stepped out on to the lawn. There stood William
Tell in full Swiss costume, yodeling and waving his
crossbow.

" 'Watch me shoot an apple off Billy's head,' he
called.

" 'Mr. Tell, Mr. Tell!' cried the Governor, 'please,
I must insist. It's dangerous!'

" 'It's all right,' shouted Tell, and began firing
arrows in the air toward Billy. It was not until he
had hit the boy in the calf of the leg that the Governor's guards were able to stop him.

"Gesler, deeply distressed, at once published an
edict in the name of his master, the Emperor, for-

bidding entirely the Swiss national pastime of shooting apples off boys' heads.

"The popular indignation over this edict is said to
have led to the revolt of the Swiss cantons."

AND IN FICTION

It has occurred to me also that the same principle
might be applied to the elucidation of our fiction.
Very often it stops just at the point where the reader
would like to know what happened next. For example—to take one random example out of an infinite
number—take the very familiar ending of a certain
type of detective story. The mystery, thanks, let us
say, to the penetrating logic and the tireless patience
of Sherlock Holmes, has been solved. Lord Bughouse's
documents, the loss of which would have carried
down the United Kingdom, have been found. The
country is safe, and with it is saved the honor of
Lord Bughouse. It is the final scene of the story. "Mr.
Holmes," said Lord Bughouse, deeply moved, "words
cannot express my obligation to you. I know that
you do not work for money, but you must at least
let me defray the expenses to which you have been
put."

After which Lord Bughouse is shown downstairs to
his Brougham, and the story ends. But it shouldn't.
There ought to be another chapter under the heading:

SHERLOCK HOLMES SENDS IN HIS BILL

There can be no doubt that if the activities of the great detective in fiction were charged up, like those of a lawyer, or an engineer, or a doctor, the cost would be high. Such as this:—

(1) Remaining in profound thought (opening chapter) at $25.00 an hour $ 50.00

(2) Forging an inexorable chain of logic, at $10.00 a link 2,000.00

(3) Intense reflection in armchair pursued apparently for six months at $30.00 an evening 5,000.00

(4) Outside activities for 6 months, including railroad fares to Constantinople and back 10,000.00

(5) Taxi Cab left with engine running in Chapter III and forgotten 15,000.00

(6) Services of 16 railway porters, 20 nightwatchmen, and 80 taxi cab drivers in gathering clues at $5.00 per day per clue 20,000.00

Total $52,050.00

"After all," said Lord Bughouse, as he wrote a check on the Treasury for the amount, "I doubt if it was worth it."

PART III

Brain Stuff in General

LIFE AND LAUGHTER

How to Infuse Our Life with the Spirit of Merriment

(NOTE: *The "piece" which follows was written for Xmas time and first published in a Canadian magazine. Hence the episodes in it are mainly taken from Canadian life and politics. But I don't know that it is any the worse for that.*)

———

EVERYBODY wishes that we could have in life more humour and more laughter; that we could "look on the bright side," "keep on smiling," "laugh off trouble," and so on. We keep on telling one another this. But no one seems to know how to go about it.

Once a year and once only we catch what seems to be the proper animating spirit, and that is at Christmas time. But how soon we lose it. At Christmas time there is a pleasant pretense, a general make-believe that we are all better than we are: and not only better, but merrier. How brightly we greet one another on Christmas morning! How transformed are our ordinary dull faces! How easily we rise above any of the petty annoyances of life. Hear us at our breakfast—

"I'm so sorry, I'm afraid the toast is cold—"

"Oh, that doesn't matter, I like it better that way."

"The poached eggs, I'm afraid, are not so good as they might be. Willie dropped his Christmas paints into them."

"Oh, that's all right."

See us, when we go to church, all bright and rosy— *"Good morning! Good morning! Glorious day, isn't it? The snow is lovely, isn't it? And the air like wine, eh? You must drop in and see us. We never seem to get together."*

All day we keep it up—our super-self, the submerged part of each of us, far beyond our common reach—and when the magic day has passed, it drops away from us. We can't hold it. The strain is too great.

But the chief reason by which we cannot keep ourselves at the Christmas level is because our sense of values is all wrong. We, the people of western civilization, have bred in ourselves, as the price of our advancement, an over-great sense of the future, an over-anxiety, an over-appreciation of ultimate purpose, an under-appreciation of immediate good. We are never quite free from the little cloud of anxiety that surrounds and follows each of us as a nimbus. Our mind is set with a background of crape. We can laugh, but you have to thump us hard to get it out of us. An Ethiopian can laugh at next to nothing. In merry Abyssinia, I imagine, they have a good time all the time. For which we go and drop bombs on them, on the ground that they don't work enough.

Of all our intellectual equipment, the thing we ought to value most, the sense of humour, the liberation that goes with laughter—we value least. We live in a prison with a door opening into a pleasant garden, and never pass through it. The garden, indeed, is walled. But so pleasantly is it grown with shrub and blossom that the wall you never see. So it is with life and laughter.

There is a story in the Greek mythology of how Pandora, the first woman, was sent to earth by Jupiter in order to perplex and disturb mankind. Among other things she was given a box from out of which flew Envy, Hatred and Malice, and all things evil. But with them at the bottom of all was Hope, which saved mankind.

The story is all right; but it would have been far better if Pandora had had *Humour* in the bottom of the box—the "saving sense" of a joke, as the true salvation of mankind.

Now let us suppose then that in these closing days of the year 1936 (in the old Greek Calendar the year 2712), Jupiter looks out again from Olympus and sees that Pandora's poor little gift of Hope had proved quite ineffectual to dry the tears of mankind. Inspired with a bright idea (he seems to have got a bright one about once every five hundred years) Jupiter sends Pandora out again, this time with a box filled with Distilled Humour, to shake and distribute throughout the world.

As a matter of fact, as any chemical scientist will tell you, we even have the preparation all ready for Pandora to use. There is a gas that is called by science, Nitrous Oxide, but nicknamed by those who know it in practice as "Laughing Gas." Take a whiff or two of it and the world all at once turns upside down into the jolliest place imaginable.

Suppose Pandora, at our Christmas time, shook the box out all over us! How marvellous! What a change at once in our politics, our public life, our society. Let us illustrate what some of the effects would be, beginning with the mightiest in the land and working downward. Let us break into the mails (who cares, in a renovated world, for a little thing like robbing the mails?) and read some of the correspondence of the great. Ha! here is an interesting item right away:

I

The Renovated Christmas Mail

From the Right Honorable R. B. Christmas Bennett to the Rev. William Spirit-of-fun Aberhart.

Dear Arb,

Sitting here laughing over the elections of last year, I've been thinking over that Social Credit stuff of yours, and I think I can begin to see far more fun in it than I did at the time. Mackenzie King and I were over in the Château Laurier today talking about that "twenty-five dollars each" and we just laughed and laughed! The new Governor-General came in and we told him, and honestly, he laughed until we thought he'd die! He says you ought to go over to England; they're too dull over there; you'd have the whole House of Lords in a roar. Let's think out some more good ones!

Still better work could be done by Pandora, if she would sprinkle a double dose of Nitrous Oxide over Geneva. The result would be something like this in the Press despatches of the next day:

II

Christmas Merriment at Geneva

Geneva (*Night before Christmas*). Fashionable Geneva never turned out in greater force than it did last night to attend the Gala Performance of Mr. John Bull, the Famous Ventriloquist, with his Talking Dolls. The scene was indeed a brilliant one inasmuch as it had been decided to use the Assembly

Hall of the League of Nations for the putting on of
the Comic Show. As Mr. Laffitoff, the delegate from
Russia, said, "How in hell can we make a better use
of it?" To which the delegate from Siam, we are told,
answered, "Eh, what, me too!" Roars of laughter
greeted the introduction of Mr. Bull on the Platform
by Signor Aloisi, who described him as a Reformed
Prize Fighter now going in for Ventriloquism. Signor
Aloisi said that he only wished his leader Mussolini
could have been present to sing his famous song "A
Life on the Ocean Wave." The house simply roared
with laughter. Somebody shouted, "What about
Hitler!" and again the house rocked with merriment.
Indeed the entire audience was filled with what may
be called the Geneva spirit and refused to take any
of the proceedings seriously.

Mr. Bull's performance was preceded by a Negro
(Ethiopian) quartet who gave a marvellously appealing rendering of: "*Way down upon the Tsana River.*"

Signor Aloisi was so moved that he said he would
like to drop a bomb on them.

Mr. John Bull's own performance as a Ventriloquist with his Talking Dolls has already enjoyed such
wide publicity as to need no detailed explanation.
Suffice it to say that Mr. Bull was in tip-top form.
His capacious person and the singularly wide spread
of his legs, encased in the familiar corduroy and
gaiters, enables Mr. Bull to hold what seems an

extraordinary number of dolls on each knee. Some of the spectators expressed the opinion that he had a doll for just about every country in the league. His performance is indeed marvellous. When Mr. Bull throws back his head, with his features absolutely immobile and his expression entirely serious, it is impossible to believe that the voice is coming from Mr. Bull and not from the doll.

"Now then, Tommy," said Mr. Bull, giving a shake to a little doll, more or less collapsed upon one of his knees, and wearing round its neck the legend, *"Tommy Lebrun, the Bon Marché Paris"*—"now then, Tommy, what is your idea?" Tommy lifted his head, or seemed to, and said *"Sanctions"*—while the entire house broke into a roar of laughter. "And now, Pedro"—continued Mr. Bull, still absolutely grave, and shaking another doll, "and how are you today?" The doll Pedro, which had a label *"Return Fare paid to Venezuelo, Second Class,"* raised itself upright, opened and shut its eyes a few times with a wide blink and said, *"I love Italy!"*

The evening was brought to a close with a little one-act play—*The White Man's Burden,* played by the entire cast of the league.

Nor is it only at Geneva that Pandora might benefit mankind. If she were to fly over to Ottawa and shake out a little Nitrous Oxide on Parliament Hill, Ottawa, our papers might carry the record of it.

III

Opening of Parliament at Ottawa

The opening session of the Parliament of Canada last month presented a scene of general hilarity scarcely equalled since Confederation. The entry of the new Governor-General was a signal for all members to rise and sing,

Do you ken John Buchan, as he was the other day,
But he's now Lord Something—it's a word that we
*   can't say.*

Equal merriment greeted the new Prime Minister, the members, both Liberal and Conservative, joining in the Christmas hymn of:

> *Hark the herald angels sing,*
> *Glory to Mackenzie King!*

The prime minister, *Sir William*, as he now is, addressed the house. Members, he said, would observe that since he had taken office he had conferred a knighthood on himself (*laughter*). He regarded this as a pretty rich joke on his right honorable friend opposite (*roars of laughter*). But he thought fit to tell the house that this knighthood would be the only one given: he himself didn't believe in them, in fact he abominated them, and nothing but his sense of humour had induced him to assume one.

He would now, he said, take up the question of the Canadian National Railway and what to do with it. (*Uproarious laughter, in which the prime minister joined.*) He would inform the house that the deficit on the rotten thing seemed bigger than ever: it was bigger on the first of December than on the first of November and in his opinion it was nothing to what it was going to be (*laughter and shouts*). Figures would be laid before the house to prove this; he himself couldn't understand them, but he didn't need to. He had now a professor in his cabinet who could do all that sort of dirty work (*cheers*). He, himself, was going to take another trip to Japan, or perhaps to Honolulu—anywhere where there was a little brighter life than here (*cheers*). He said that the budget would be brought down presently—that is sometime—he himself couldn't make head or tail of it, but if members would only leave things alone everything would be all right. He ended—so far as the Hansard reporters could get his words in the tumult of laughter—by telling the members to go to Hull.

When Pandora had finished with nations and parliaments she might turn her attention to the world of learning and brighten up our colleges with a little laughing gas. No more angry recriminations back and forward! No more complaints of the students that the professors are senile! No more complaints of the trustees that the students are bolsheviks! Not a bit. Listen to this, as a result of Pandora's visit:

IV

Chancellor Corrects False Impression

A distinct contribution to what one may call World Renovation was made by the Chancellor of one of the greatest Canadian Universities in a speech to the students before dismissing them to their Christmas vacation. The Chancellor said that, a little while ago, he had been wrongly reported in the press, or at least so it seemed to him now—in connection with a speech made by him in another university. The speech was made as a denunciation of the spread of socialism and communism in the Canadian colleges, especially among the younger professors and the more ignorant students. The Chancellor was certain that he never said this. He certainly could not have used the phrase "the more ignorant of the students." If anybody could show him any students more ignorant than the others were, he'd be glad to see them (*applause*). As to communism, he said we couldn't get too much of it. Nothing was more calculated to brighten up our colleges than a little wholesome revolution. In regard to the professors, he was glad that some of them at any rate had a little touch of youth about them. He looked round, he said, at the bunch of them in his employ and they looked a pretty rickety lot. But he could assure his young friends that means would be taken to get rid of most of them (*applause*). Last year quite a few died (*cheers*): with luck a lot would drop this year.

But—the Chancellor added—why talk of *education* in a college. He would rather say a few words about the big game between Varsity and McGill last year that practically settled the Rugby championship. He had seldom seen finer and cleaner play and had realized when he looked at it that what we need at our Canadian colleges is more fun and lots of it!

But this renovated spirit can penetrate into even darker places than colleges and parliaments. I can imagine it invading even the criminal courts, the unknown domain from the very thought of which most of us turn with a shudder. I have a friend, a Chief Justice, one of the best, the kindliest, the wittiest of men. So nature made him. Yet there he has to sit in his criminal court and send people into the dark. If he could give way to the promptings of his own heart, or if Pandora might drop into his court some of the Tear Gas of Laughter of which we spoke, how different it might be. Witness this:

V

Scene: *The Chief Justice and the Burglar*

THE CHIEF JUSTICE (*looking at his notes*) — "You are accused here, it seems, of breaking into the house. Is that correct?"

THE PRISONER — "Yes."

"And you broke in *at night*, why *at night*? Can't you see that that is what aggravates your offense?"

"I had to break in at night" (*said the prisoner*) — "in the day, the dog was there."

"Oh, there was a dog?"

"Yes, one of those infernal police-dogs."

"Ah, well" (*said the judge*), "that's different, I don't blame you for that. I hate those infernal brutes myself. I can quite understand that in that case you would come at night. But, look, you climbed up and got into this man's house, into his study, by a first story window. That's bad. Why didn't you go in by the door?"

"I couldn't get in. I had a skeleton key but the door had one of those narrow locks you can't see in the dark."

"Those things!" (*said the judge*) "yes, awful, aren't they? I have one on my front door: simply impossible to find! Well, that makes that clear. You couldn't get in at the door so you climbed up to the window. Then you got in, it seems, and took his money off the table. Why?"

"I needed it. I'd been cleaned out at bridge the night before and either I had to have that money or I'd have lost my game."

"You play bridge?" asked the judge eagerly.

"Oh, yes, every day!"

"So do I. What do you think of the three diamonds convention—I mean after trumps are led?"

"No use for it. I think it spoils the game. In fact, I'm against conventions at all."

THE CHIEF JUSTICE (*with enthusiasm*)—"Exactly, just my own idea. Now let's settle this other business. First, it seems you came to this man's house at night because the fellow kept a dog there all day, couldn't get in because of his wretched, unworkable lock, you climbed to his room, found him out and took his money off the table in order so as not to miss your game of bridge. It seems from the record that you are a college man, and this man I understand is not, but has made a pile of money in business. The whole thing seems clear now: The case, if there ever was one, is dismissed and if you have no other engagement, will you drop down to the University Club and have a game? I'd like to try out what you say about the conventions."

And the Chief Justice, as he left the court, deep in thought, realized, that if you see the world with proper vision, you can understand everything and forgive everything.

THE HIDDEN SECRET OF THE CITY

That It Still Dreams of the Farm

EVERY year when the good old summertime begins I feel that longing to turn my back—all of it—on the city, which is probably felt by nine city dwellers out of ten. Not for me the roar of the metropolis. Let me feel the new-mown hay blow in my face and let me hear the trout stream gurgle under the fallen logs in the bush. I know all that can be said in favor of the city. I admit that it palpitates with intellectual life, that it throbs with the conscious power of collective thought. But not for me—not a palpitation, not a throb!

The truth is, and I don't mind admitting it at this time of year, I am afraid, and always have been, of a great city and of the kind of people who live in it. Like everybody else who has come off a farm—our homestead was in Georgina Township, up in Ontario; perhaps you know it?—I have never felt at ease with high class city people, with financial magnates, great criminal lawyers, bank presidents and scintillating literary wits. I always felt that the wits might start something or the magnates sit on something or the great criminal lawyer might say something. Anybody

from the country knows the feeling. As to the
bankers, everybody knows that these men hold the
world in the hollow of their hand; if they lift their
thumb over we go. So I am uneasy with them. I don't
want them to lift it while I'm round.

But that feeling is all gone since an experience I
had just a little while ago. It was my fate to have to
give an address at one of the biggest luncheon clubs
on the *Diplomatic Situation in Europe,* in one of the
biggest hotels of one of our cities before some of the
biggest men in the country. If anything sounds bigger than that, I don't hear it. It was certainly a distinguished crowd. As I looked round at the vast
glittering hotel dining-room, filled with hundreds
and hundreds of what I knew were typical city
men, leaders in business and finance and the profes-
sions, I felt appalled. It seemed impossible that I
could dare to speak to them.

So there I sat, at the head of the table, in the very
centre of that marvellous gathering, making conversation as best I could. Beside me was the president
of one of the biggest banks in the world, a fine, dignified man who looked the part. I wouldn't have
dared to borrow $5 from him, if I was dying.

I talked as best I could; and presently, by chance,
I mentioned Ohio. "I come from there," he said, and
then added, as if owning up to something, like an
honest man, "we had a farm there; as a matter of

fact, I have it still." The moment he said that I felt easier. "Did you?" I said. "I was brought up on a farm in Ontario—Georgina Township—we had a hundred acres, counting the bush." "We had more than that," said the bank president; "we had over five hundred"—then he realized, like the kindly man he is, that he had said a rather brutal thing, as between farmers, and he added at once: "Of course, the old homestead wasn't as much as that at first; we only had a quarter section less sixty acres. But later when Uncle Bill went out West we had his half section, less the road allowance of four rods that went right across the place just behind the homestead."

The words were like music! "Quarter sections" and "homesteads," and relations called "Uncle Bill," and things measured in "rods"! That's the language I like to hear! I felt at home at once.

With that we were started. Five minutes later, if the conversation of that great financier had been reported, it would have run like this: "You can do better with soy beans for hogs than you can in trying to raise grain for them. Put in your soy beans, with a cover crop first—"

But I had to interrupt him there. "Soy beans are all right," I said, "if the land is clean enough." And with that we were absorbed; gone was all the glitter and the form and pomp of the occasion. The bank president was back in Ohio and I was back in

Georgina Township (next to North Gwillimbury, you can't miss it; take the town line past the old Prosser place) and he was feeding hogs on soy beans, and I was objecting that if he didn't raise any wheat he'd have no straw for bedding, and he admitted it. Think of a man in his position sleeping on straw!

All of a sudden I remembered, we both seemed to remember, where we were. Imagine talking farm stuff in a gathering like that! And in the silence that fell for the moment between us, I listened and caught a little of the talk of the group of men—presidents of this, and vice-presidents of that—who sat at the table just beneath the head table that was ours. One man I noticed in particular, a dignified figure, the face of a diplomat. He was saying to the man beside him: "Don't talk to me of leghorn hens! I won't have them on my place. You waste your money in trying to put a twelve-foot wire fence round a leghorn, and even then they'll fly over it. No, sir, I admit they lay, but give me a heavy fowl, a Barred Rock or a Black Jersey Giant, and you've got something! They'll lay pretty good, and they're a table bird and you don't have to chase them all over the place!"

"But wait a minute," objected the man next to him. "You can't make them pay!"

I listened, fascinated! They were talking of that wonderful, vital question, "Can hens be made to pay?"

"They do pay!" said the first man. "Out at my place in Indiana last week we showed a clear profit on them!"

He didn't say how much: no one was cruel enough to ask. But I knew, because my hens back in Ontario have been showing a clear profit right along, a total of sixty cents in November (and mind, I've only two hundred hens) and eight cents in December and this last month over a dollar! So I understood just what was meant. That banker, I suppose, wouldn't take any special joy in a corporation that would pay a dividend on $5,000,000; but to make a profit, an actual profit, on hens (not counting, of course, your own time, nor the hired man's time, nor the odd months when they don't lay)— Ah! that is high finance!

So after that I felt easier. And when I realized that my neighbour on the left was talking about trout fishing in an Indiana creek, and the man next him was spearing suckers with a jack light, then it was all too easy.

So when I got up to speak I knew that I was among friends, men whose thoughts I could share, whose sympathies I could call forth.

"In rising, gentlemen," I said, "to speak on this matter of the Diplomatic Situation in Europe, I find myself in no little difficulty. I have just come down here from my farm—a little place that I call my farm—in Simcoe County, Ontario, where I have, gentlemen, nearly ten acres, without counting two acres of bush."

I could feel a distinct wave of interest pass over the audience. They seemed to draw their chairs sympathetically nearer to me.

"Yes, gentlemen," I continued, "ten acres and a little bush. The bush, I admit, is mostly soft maple and ash with a little black birch, and I know that you will at once tell me that you don't call that first-class hard wood. No, neither do I. But it is easy to cut, gentlemen, and you can get in there with your portable saw most any time. But, as I say, in regard to this Diplomatic Situation in Europe, I went up to my place then—it's just off the Muskoka Highway; if any of you come up ask at Hatley's store—to work up this question, and I found it hard to do so. You see, gentlemen, we had, in our section, as no doubt you had, a rather mean spring this year—an early thaw that took off the snow and that sharp frost that winter-killed a lot of the fall wheat."

All over the audience I could see men nodding in confirmation. "It hit the apple trees hard, gentlemen; I lost about half a dozen MacIntosh red, just coming nicely into bearing. I know you'll at once all ask me why I hadn't banked them up with manure in the fall. Well, I'll tell you, gentlemen, I don't believe in it. No, sir!"

I could sense sensation, denial and corroboration rippling all round among the audience.

"I hold that if you bank up your young trees that way, you *soften* them. They lose body and the fruit is never really firm; and, what's more, gentlemen, you have all kinds of bugs, as you know, getting round your roots. Well, I wouldn't enlarge on it!"

I could hear a sigh of disappointment.

"All I'm saying," I went on, "is that what with one thing and another there was too much to do round the place to let me get at this question of the Diplomatic Situation in Europe, on which I was invited here to address you. You know how crowded a man gets on a little place like that, especially just at seeding time with everything coming on at once. You haven't the leisure, the spare time, of city folks. And then I was specially anxious, gentlemen, as soon as the spell of really fine weather should set in, I was specially anxious to have another try at early cucumbers. I don't know whether any of you gentlemen have ever tried early cucumbers—"

Had they? I could see by the thrill of excitement, the tenseness of this luncheon audience, that they all had!

"But if you *have*, then you know that early cucumbers are a mighty speculative thing! It takes nerve! One nasty frost and you may lose a dozen plants at a crack. You don't feel safe, at least not up with us, not clear through till the first of June. You can start them all right, that's not the trouble, I admit, but it's when you come to *set them out!*"

They were listening, breathless.

"The gentleman sitting next to me but one—who is, I understand, a member of your State Senate—says he does fairly well with his cucumbers by starting them in a greenhouse. He says that last year he had eight, or was it nine, really fine plants, started that way, though he admits he took a lot of trouble with them. But I don't think, gentlemen, that you'll ever the flavour in a cucumber started in a greenhouse. Now, I'll tell you my plan—and I give it you for what it's worth."

There was tense excitement now all over the audience.

"You take an old sod and cut it with your jack-knife into about a four-inch square, turn it upside down and put your seed into that!"

Sensation!

"Then take your sods and set them in rows in a hot bed with lots of first-class manure, gentlemen—and I know I need not tell men like you that when I say manure, I mean real manure with lots of body, not just a lot of dry straw. You want heat. But I need not tell men like you what manure is. Use lots of it and tramp it well down, till you're satisfied. Give it a four-inch layer of the best dirt you can lay your hands on, put your sods on, and you'll get real results.

"But what I mean about this Diplomatic Situation in Europe is that I didn't get time to work it up; in fact, to be quite frank, I'll go so far as to say that I don't give a damn about it anyway! I'd rather be up on my ten-acre farm setting out cucumbers than loafing round all the Chancelleries of Europe, or whatever they call them—and unless I am much mistaken, so would you, every one of you!"

There was deafening applause. They said it was one of the finest talks they'd heard for years. And later the reporters of the papers—you know how clever those boys are—had it all fixed up under the heading *"Home Agricultural Interest First Claim on Nation,"* and so I saw what I had really meant.

But meantime I had drifted out of the place and over to one of the big city clubs, feeling pretty well elated. Till now, though my friends have often been kind enough to put me up, I've been afraid to go into those metropolitan Clubs. But this time I walked into the lounge-room of one of the swellest of them with absolute confidence. I was beginning to understand the city.

It was the quiet hour of the club day, the early afternoon. There was hardly anyone in the lounge except a couple of ministers—clergymen. I knew what they were by their quiet black dress and their

kind serious faces. One of them, I could see by his
gaiters, must be an Episcopal bishop. I didn't want to
overhear their talk, as I felt sure it would deal with
some of their spiritual ministrations, and be, in a
way, private. But I couldn't help it. The Bishop was
saying:

"Then just as she seemed to be getting along so
well, something went wrong." He paused and shook
his head and repeated "something went wrong!"

"Till then," the other asked anxiously, "she had
seemed quite all right?"

"Quite," said the Bishop. "Quite! A little restless,
perhaps, at times. But then I thought that meant
merely that the flies were troubling her. She'd been
giving eight to ten quarts every morning and at least
six at night. . . ."

"Perhaps," said the other in gentle admonishment,
"perhaps you put her on the grass too early?"

"She hadn't been on the grass," said the Bishop
slowly, and added with a groan, "We were still feeding her chop!"

There was a pause, I could see that they were old
friends, and that argument was painful to them, yet
the lesser clergyman said firmly, "I know we mustn't
dispute it again; but don't you think, perhaps, that
Holsteins—I say it with all gentleness . . ."

I rose and moved quietly away. I knew that they
were going to talk of the unsolved problem of the

Holstein versus the Jersey cow, beside which squaring the circle is child's play: but I couldn't bear to hear it; our last little Jersey—but no, no, never mind. The country, too, like the city, has its sharp tragedies.

.   .   .   .

So now, I know the city and I'm not afraid of it. I understand city men. As they sit in their palatial hotels they are dreaming of morning mists rising off the pasture in the river valley. As they study at their meals their bills of fare, they are not looking at such items as Pâté Bourgignon à la Marengo, which the Chef sticks on the list to remind himself of France. What they are trying to find is Flop-Over pancakes, Honey, and Liver and Bacon à la Wabash. And when the orchestra starts its softest music, they'll close their eyes and hear the drone of the cow-bells in the bush.

The Great City! There's no such place. It's just where people go, bravely enough, to earn the money to get back home.

I know now that I can go down to Wall Street, New York, with a bag of soy beans under one arm and a hen under the other, and borrow all the money I want.

NEW LIGHT FROM BRIGHT MINDS

When You Want to Learn Something Ask Those Who Don't Know. The Idea Is Simple and Should Have Been Thought of Before.

PEOPLE who read the newspapers regularly must have noticed that the reported interviews are getting to be much brighter and more interesting than they used to be. Until recently, when the reporters interviewed travellers, distinguished visitors and political emissaries, they talked to each of them about his own particular line of life and the things about which he was supposed to know something. The result was fearful dullness.

Nowadays the thing is done in exactly the other way. Each distinguished visitor is asked questions about something that is outside of his own line of life. A vaudeville comedian gives his impression of French politics and an English bishop gives his views of women's skirts.

The result is a freshness and a charm which lend a new attraction to our newspapers on both sides of the Atlantic.

Here are a few examples taken from the current

press and drawn, as appears at once, indifferently from England and America.

I

Ball Player Visits St. Paul's

London, Friday—Ed Lanigan, star outfielder and manager of the Tuscaloosa Baseball Nine, passed through London this morning and expressed himself as delighted with it. After he had had a run round town, Ed gave his views, at the Hotel Piccadilly, to a crowd of assembled admirers on some of the things he had seen.

"What did you think of St. Paul's, Ed?" asked one of the boys.

"It's certainly big stuff," said Ed, "and it gets me. Those old guys certainly knew how to build. And I want to tell you boys right now that there's something about that building that you don't get every day. I doubt if there are a dozen men in New York today who could duplicate it."

"How does the political situation in England strike you?" he was next queried.

"Fine!" answered the big man. "They've sure got a lot of taxes here. But then, mind you, there's a lot of wealth too. Of course things are pretty bad, but you've got to remember they were bad before, and, anyway, they're not so bad."

II

Movie Star Sees Riviera

Gus Phinn, the well-known movie star, who is said to command a salary of anywhere above half a million dollars, was a recent visitor at Mentone. Gus is enthusiastic over the Mediterranean Sea.

"I want to tell you right now," he said to a representative of the press, "that there is absolutely nothing wrong with the Mediterranean."

"What did you specially notice about it, Gus?" asked the reporter.

"Why, what gets me hardest is the color of the water. Say, I don't think you can beat that blue anywhere. You might try, but you can't do it."

"Do you think," asked another of the group, "that the tone of English social life is deteriorating?"

"No, I don't," Gus replied. "I think the tone is good. I think it A-1."

"What about the relations of England and France, Gus?"

"They're all right," the star answered. "We met a lot of French boys on the boat, and certainly nicer boys you wouldn't want to meet."

III

Copper King Looks at Oxford

E. J. Slagg, the multimillionaire owner of mines and president of Slagg Consolidated Copper, visited Oxford yesterday and was shown round the colleges. The big copper man, whose quiet taciturnity and power of silence have made him the terror of the Stock Exchange, looked about him at everything with the same keen shrewdness with which he detects a vein of copper under a hundred feet of traprock. Only now and then he darted a shrewd question or let fall a short comment.

"This place," he said, "is old." On the threshold of the Bodleian Library he paused a moment as if rapidly measuring the contents with his eye.

"Mostly books?" he asked.

The copper king also paused a moment before the monument erected to the memory of Latimer and Ridley.

"What's the idea?" he asked. . . .

But, as I said up above, this new and brilliant flood of light is not only turned on Europe. By a similar process it is let loose on the American continent too:

IV

British Lord Sees Jersey Tugs

Lord Tinklepin, who arrived from England on the
Aquitania yesterday, was taken for a trip up and
down the harbor in a fast tug. His lordship expressed
himself as amazed at the commerce of New York.
"I had no idea of it," he said.

Passing by one of the car ferries of the Erie Railroad, Lord Tinklepin expressed the keenest interest.
"What the devil is that?" he asked. On being told
what it was, the distinguished visitor, who is well
known for his interest in physical science, at once
asked, "Why doesn't it upset?"

V

Lady Visitor on American Banks

Lady Mary Messabout, president of the Women's
Federation for Universal Mutual Understanding, was
shown round financial New York yesterday as the
guest of the Bankers' Association. Lady Mary expressed the greatest wonder at the Sub-Treasury of
the United States.

"Is it possible," she said, "that it's full of money?"
Lady Mary was questioned by representatives of
the press as to her opinion of the American banking
system.

"It is really excellent," she answered, "so little delay and such civility everywhere."

"Do you think"—it was asked by a member of the press—"that the deflation of American currency would check the expansion of business?"

"Oh, I hope not," Lady Mary answered warmly; "surely it would never do that."

VI

French Baron Visits West

The Baron de Vieux Château, who is visiting Saskatchewan with a view to seeing whether the richer parts of Canada would be suited for the poorer class of Frenchmen, was taken yesterday on a tour of inspection of the grain elevators of Saskatoon.

"But they are marvelous!" the Baron said to a member of the press on his return to his hotel. "They seem to me absolutely—how shall I say it?—enormous."

When asked what was his impression of the Farmers' Coöperative Movement, the distinguished visitor again spoke with enthusiasm. "But your farmers!" he said, "they are wonderful! What courage! What tenacity! To have come here and stayed here! It is wonderful."

THE PERSONAL HABITS AND SAYINGS OF
THE EMPEROR NAPOLEON

As Advertised

WHY are there so few great men? Perhaps it has occurred to you, dear reader, to wonder why so few men succeed in raising themselves above the average level? Or perhaps it hasn't. Very few things seem to occur to you anyhow. But if it did you would ask yourself why cannot we all raise ourselves above the average? The answer is, very simply, that we all can if we try.

In short, anybody who wishes to take a long step forward in the success movement should study the lives and careers of great men. And he should not study them in the dull pages of the college histories. There, only a very partial and limited account is found. He should study them in the much more human and vivid records supplied in the advertising pages of the success magazines. For example, it is very doubtful whether Bancroft ever knew that George Washington was in the habit of taking four deep breaths just before eating. If he did he never mentions it. Nor does he make any reference to the fact that Benjamin Franklin once said that no perfect breakfast food had as yet been found (that, of course, was in his day; it has been found since, as we shall see). In the same way Lord Macaulay, a man otherwise well informed, does not seem to know that Oliver Cromwell once said the secret of making money lies in scientific investment. Nor was Shakespeare aware that the cloak or mantle which Julius Caesar wore on the day he overcame the Nervii and which he wore when he was stabbed by his assassins was undoubtedly made by the famous Knit-Right process, now so widely known.

In short, as a result of the wonder movement of success, the whole of our history is being rewritten. We are getting to know things about our great men which we never knew before—intimate, personal things that we never knew before.

And of all the historical characters whose careers are being thus illuminated, there is one who stands out conspicuously above all others—the Emperor Napoleon.

This great man enjoys in the success movement an eminence over all others. It is the aim of everybody to be a Napoleon in his own particular line of activity, and a great many are succeeding. You can see their pictures any day. There are at least thirty-seven Napoleons now doing business. There is a "Napoleon of Billiards," and a "Napoleon of Water Polo," and a "Napoleon of the Rubber Shoe Industry," and there is also a man who is the "Napoleon of Pants Designers," and another who is the "Napoleon of the Ladies' Shirtwaist Business." There is a dog who is the Napoleon of Airedale Terriers, and there is a cow who is the Napoleon of Holstein milk-givers.

In short, it is becoming a very important thing to learn how to be a Napoleon.

You have only to turn over the back pages of any of our greatest journals—the serious pages where they teach people how to live and how to sell things —to see little pictures of Napoleon inserted everywhere. Sometimes there is just his head under his hat; sometimes a full-length picture to show his hands clasped behind his back. And in each case there is some little motto which Napoleon said or some statement about his habits. From beyond the years and over the wastes of the South Atlantic, Napoleon is still teaching us how to live and how to sell things.

From these statements thus printed I have pieced together a composite picture of Napoleon in which are shown those little personal things which made him what he was.

Anybody who wants to be a Napoleon has only to imitate these things. I admit that they are a little complicated. But even Napoleon couldn't have learned them all at once. He must have picked them up bit by bit.

In the first place, the great Emperor was an early

riser. The hour of three in the morning saw him in the saddle or at his desk. "Early rising," he once said when talking of a well-known breakfast food, "not only peptonizes the stomach, but with the aid of a simple remedy obtained at all drug stores, restores tone and vigor to the lost digestion."

Napoleon also sat up late. He never sought his couch till three in the morning. "The later the hour," he once said, in referring to a new patent oil lamp, "the better the brain."

It was the practice of Napoleon to chew his food twenty minutes before swallowing it. Eating a sirloin steak took him all day. Napoleon was in the habit of eating standing up. He also ate lying down. He could even sit and eat.

Before coming to any great decision Napoleon always made a point of taking four deep breaths through his nose. While talking the great Emperor habitually kept his mouth firmly shut.

Napoleon always wore wool next to his skin. He once said, in an interview which he seems to have given to a well-known firm of woolen manufacturers in Paterson, New Jersey, "There is nothing like wool."

In the same way he always said, "There is nothing like a delicious cup of Ozo when exhausted from the pulpit and the platform."

Napoleon drank, but always with the strictest

avidity.

Napoleon made little use of tobacco except in the form of snuff or cigars or cut plug.

During his exile at St. Helena Napoleon is reported to have said, "If I had taken a course in Personal Leadership, I should not have landed here."

PART IV

Nation and Nation

THIS INTERNATIONAL STUFF

For Men Like Myself

TODAY, out in my garden picking peas, I found myself thinking about the ominous situation in Europe and everywhere, and the fact that at any time noisy cities and quiet countrysides may be devastated by war. I use the tall kind of peas that grow from five to six feet high; it takes the birds longer to get them; often you have some left.

But they grow so high that you sit in the shade of them. And when they are staked up they look something like the long rows of vines along the valleys of the Rhine and the Danube and the Yangtze Kiang and in all the soft sunny corners of the earth where people are soon going to kill one another, if one believes the headlines. So I thought of all the people everywhere tending the vines, and planting the red brown fields, all warm with sun and nature's happiness, but in a short time to be turned loose— no one knows why—to kill one another. They don't want to—any more than I do.

I'd kill a crow—any gardener would—but I wouldn't kill an Australian or a Hungarian. I'd rather have the Hungarian make *goulash;* in fact I think without exaggeration, rather than kill him, I'd eat it. And yet, perhaps this summer, regiments of furious cavalry will be shouting *Goulash! Goulash!* as they charge on the enemy; and the enemy will answer defiantly with the yell *Chile con Carne!* or *Chianti!* or *Vive le Fromage de Brie!* Then the crazy pretense that nations hate one another will be turned by bloodshed into unbelievable reality.

The truth is that the world has long since outgrown nationalism, and yet we don't seem to realize it. National isolation, national war, national exclusiveness, are in reality things of the past. Every art and mechanism of our economic life, our manufacture, our transport, our flights in the clouds, our voices in the ether of space, all proclaim the unity of the globe. Everything has been unified—except man himself.

What the world needs now is internationally minded men—I'll put it very simply—men like myself. You ask, where on earth can you get them? I admit it's hard.

In my own case, I really feel that I am an internationally minded man. I have no prejudices. As a Canadian, I am willing to admit, if you like, that perhaps the Canadians are just a little bit bigger and brainier than any other people. But then the Americans to the south of us are a mighty fine people, and even over in Europe and Asia and Africa there are a lot of fine people, too.

I met a little feller from Europe the other day—a Croat, or a Chick, or a Slick, or something. Where was it he said he came from? Toschen or Poschen—anyway, somewhere. And he seemed all right, a nice little feller. So they all do.

How often do you hear people say, "I met a German and he seemed all right," "I met a New Zealander and he seemed fine," "I met a Norwegian and I couldn't see anything wrong with him." Of course not. There's nothing wrong with any of them.

All the people of the world, taken by and large, are mighty fine people, with energy and kindness and love, valuing just the same things that we do, with the same care for their children and their friends, and their home town. All these things we value, they value.

The international man (my kind, the kind we need more of) is able to enter into the patriotism and pride of the history of other peoples, to admire and value what they have done in the past, to look with veneration at the tattered flags that recall their battles, and to thrill at the music of their national airs.

A year or so ago I was at a great gathering of one of the big service clubs of the world. And as a part of the pageant of the occasion, they had a march of delegates from different states and nations, with their flags and music.

I watched a detachment from New England marching by to the sound of *When Johnny Comes Marching Home Again, Hurrah! Hurrah!* and I thought to myself, "That's the stuff! The real old Massachusetts spirit, you can't beat that," and I felt that the one place nearest my heart (being international) was old New England.

But the next minute another crowd burst into sight, with a band playing, *Way Down South in Dixie,* and with Texas Rangers in sombrero hats and Louisiana Tigers all ready for a spring. Then I could feel my heart move south of Mason and Dixon's line, and throb at the glory of the Lost Cause.

I could even feel a southern accent rising on my tongue—till just at that moment I heard the *skirl* of the bagpipes—you can't even pronounce *skirl* unless you live north of the Clyde—and the music, or rather the sound of *The Campbells are coming, er-er, er-er!!* and I saw the kilts and bonnets of bonny Scotland— the grrreatest country in the world! I thought to myself, where can you get another country to compare with Scotland?

But the question answered itself a minute later as the next detachment passed in a torrent of tossing emerald green and a band that loudly called with drum and fife to ask, *Oh! Denis Dear, and Did You Hear the News That's Going Round?*

But if you think the Scotch or the Irish an inspiring sight, wait till you see what a detachment of French, the most martial nation in the world, can look like, all tanned and brown with the Algerian sun, all dingy red and dusty blue with a march step that has in it the precision of centuries, the prestige of the great wars, rising and falling in tune to the music of *Madelon! Madelon! Madelon!* . . . Even the English walking as if at a funeral to the music of *Nearer My God to Thee,* and the Canadians never quite keeping step and trying to sing the words of *Oh! Canada*—which they never quite remember—are impressive and inspiring by their very lack and scorn of sentiment.

Anyone looking at such a pageant as this—duplicated every day, for those who can see it, in the life and art of our time—ought to feel the wish to be an international man, to take his part in welding the world together so that no discord can break it asunder.

How do we do it? Well, I can tell at least a good way not to do it, and that is the method that the world has been following, the method of compacts and covenants and scraps of paper and naval agreements—otherwise disagreements. These things only accentuate national differences, only emphasize national inequalities, and instigate national wars.

"Rules of war" is a contradiction in terms. The only proper rule of war is to say that we pledge ourselves never to use any kind of weapon or any kind of attack which we don't think is the kind of weapon or the kind of attack we care to use. That hits the point to a nicety.

There was, long ago, a dear old melodrama of New England life in which an angry old-fashioned farmer, protesting at his daughter's getting "new-fangled" ideas, exclaimed, "I don't want my daughter to read no books that I don't want her to read." The speech always got a laugh. But in reality the man said just what he meant, and the diplomats would do well to follow his precept. A naval agreement should read, "We aren't going to build any ships bigger than what we feel we want to build, and we won't build any greater number than the number that we're going to build."

With a distinct understanding like that, the world could stop being preoccupied and obsessed with facts and treaties and the peace and war question, and could just go on living.

What is needed is for people to know one another, to cultivate every relationship that runs crosswise of international lines, to read one another's books, to admire one another's art, to taste one another's foods. Bring me *Caviar* and I'll eat it; fetch me *Ravioli* and I'll get it down, yes, even that South American stuff, what is it, *Chile con Carne*—I forget—anyway, I'll consume it. I'll eat *Wiener Schnitzel* with the Ger-

to do in a national crisis. Baldwin went north to shoot grouse and came back and said he had hit one. The public was reassured and kept him in office. They say he's going rook-shooting next time.

To this discussion I append two illustrative examples. The first one below under the title of *Finding a Formula* is taken from the recent memoirs of a well-known diplomat whom I will simply designate Lord X. Well-informed readers will guess at once that X is not the true name of this distinguished man. The other example, entitled the *Brown Jones Embroglio* is intended to illustrate the great benefits that would result if the private disagreements of Mr. Brown and Mr. Jones were conducted with proper diplomatic form.

I

Finding a Formula

(From the Memoirs of a Celebrated Diplomat, So Well Known That to Mention His Real Name Would Start a War)

Looking back over forty years of diplomatic experience, I can see that it was a very pleasant life that we led at dear old Geneva. Geneva, I always prefer to call it, though some of the boys (we were a highly international crowd) called it Genf or simply Gimp, or Guff. International they were, indeed, and yet some of the best fellows that ever signed a protocol or decoded a forty-eight-hour ultimatum. There was Billy Pantechnicas, the Greek ambassador, Lord Fud from England, the Italian Marchese di Malo Chianti, and a lot more. Our life, I say, was pleasant, good fun most of the time. But of course there was lots of work in it as well—drawing up protocols, and modus vivendis and ultimatums. Many a time after playing bridge till three in the morning I would go home to sit down and work on a modus vivendi till breakfast time; and even then very likely the chief would come into my room and throw down a bundle of papers and say, "Find out a formula for that, will you?" And I'd have to work for the rest of the day. If one failed to find a formula then most likely two nations would get into an *impasse,* and anything might happen. Casual readers of the newspaper when they read such an item as that Italy is trying to find a "formula" which will satisfy Turkey and yet not be too hard to guess have little idea of the desperate struggles involved.

That was our bugbear, our nightmare at dear old Gimp, the fear of an *impasse.* It was a fear that never left us.

So you can imagine what my feelings were when one morning, along in the year 1932 or 1933, Lord Fud came into my office with a face as white as *carte blanche*, flopped into a chair and gasped out:

"There's an impasse!"

"Good heavens," I said, "an impasse!"

"Yes," he repeated, "an impasse."

In diplomacy we always repeated everything three times to prevent error.

"Is it likely to embroil all Europe?" I gasped.

"It is half broiled right now," groaned Lord Fud.

"You mean that England will inevitably be drawn in?"

He nodded.

A sudden thought filled me with apprehension.

"The United States?" I asked.

"In," he answered, repeating his groan. We were both silent for a while. Then I tried to pull myself together. It might not be too late.

"Fud," I said, "we must see what can be done. We mustn't give up hope. Think of what diplomacy has already done; think of The Hague, of Locarno, of Monte Carlo—"

"That's right," he said, gathering courage, "and of Salonica, and Portsmouth, New Hampshire."

"And Ottawa, Ontario," I said. "Can't you think of any others?"

"I don't need to," he answered, "I feel better."

"All right," I continued, "now let's face the thing as it is. To begin with, where's this impasse?"

Lord Fud took out his little pocket atlas and put

on his eyeglasses.

"Inner Thibet," he said, "and Outer Kurdistan."

"Give me the book," I said. "Which page?"

"Page seventy-one."

"Seventy-one," I repeated. "It certainly looks pretty tough. It's so far off, so disconnected." I was thinking the thing out with all the power of brain I could apply to it; but I couldn't get enough.

"Don't you see," said Lord Fud, "that impasse will drag in China?"

"Inevitably," I admitted.

"Then China draws in Japan, Japan draws in Russia, Russia draws Europe, and Europe draws America."

"In other words," I said, "we are faced with a war between Europe, Asia, Africa, and America."

He nodded.

"In that case," I concluded, rising, "we must act without delay. We must find a formula. You remember, Fud, how we saved Italy last year by finding a formula; you remember the formula that broke the Polish-Silesian impasse?—a quite simple one after all. We'll have to find the formula."

"And how?" he said.

"I don't know yet," I replied, "we must ask round among the different chancelleries of Europe. Have you forgotten the chancelleries? Telegraph at once to the Quai d'Orsay, call up the Ballplatz. You're getting rusty, old boy, if you forget the Ballplatz."

"No, no," he said, "that's right—the Ballplatz, and get in touch, of course, with the Yildiz Kiosk."

"And the Wilhelmstrasse," I added, "and the Tsun-li-Yamen." In a few moments we were filled with enthusiasm. Was there time? Could we within twenty-four hours find a formula that would conciliate the claims of Outer Kurdistan and Inner Thibet?

The wires were kept busy. People who know diplomacy merely from the newspaper, I repeat, have no idea of the intense and anxious work entailed in getting a formula. They merely read at their breakfast table that Mr. Stanley Baldwin, or President Lebrun, or the American Secretary of State has found a "formula" and that everything is all right. The desperate search, the tense anxiety, they never know.

At ten o'clock that morning the formulas began to come over the wire. But to our intense disappointment, as formula after formula came in, not one seemed to suit.

The first formula that reached us was

$$x^2 - y^2 = (x + y) \ (x - y)$$

I knew at once we couldn't use it: not snappy enough.

Then came another, painfully decoded word by

word. (Remember that every one of these formulas had to be decoded.) This one, in a specially guarded cipher, came in from Washington. When at last transcribed, it read:

Take one pint of Italian Vermouth, one pint of dry gin, and one spoonful of grenadine; mix and shake over cracked ice and serve cold.

We saw at once that it wouldn't do: it was the formula for a Martini cocktail, and we had used it already in four big international difficulties.

"Won't do," said Fud disconsolately. "They know that one already."

Meantime with every hour the impasse was rapidly spreading from Asia to Europe. In spite of all the efforts of trained diplomacy it seemed impossible to check its advance. By noon it had reached the frontiers of Austria. By three o'clock it was reported in Switzerland. At five o'clock it covered all Western Europe.

At half-past five Lord Fud broke in on me in great excitement.

"There's one chance left," he said, "I've just thought of it—a conversation."

"A conversation!" At once I saw its possibilities and wondered why he had not thought of it sooner.

All the world realizes, of course, that very often

in our diplomatic work what cannot be done by direct formal means can be done by means of informal conversations. For example, again and again the peace of Europe has been saved by getting in a timely "conversation" between the foreign minister of France, the British prime minister, and one or two other dignitaries. The press never gives out details. It merely says that there has been a conversation.

I saw at once the brilliance of the idea.

"Where shall we have it?" I asked.

"What do you say to Monte Carlo?" said Fud. "Yes, or wait a bit, what about the Golf Club at Deauville?"

"Or the Jockey Club at Biarritz. Have they a license?" I asked.

"I think so," said Fud; "but if you think that point important let's hold it in Henry's American Bar, Rue Volney."

"Excellent," said I, "let's get them there."

Our action was as swift as our thoughts. I shall never forget the tense excitement as we called up Mr. Stanley Baldwin, Mussolini, and the Queen of the Netherlands and asked, "Can you fellows all come together for a conversation at Henry's? Yes, yes, at our expense—costs you nothing."

That evening while the world slept, humming aeroplanes gathered them in Paris.

What happened there—except that we started them with *canapé aux anchois* with white wine and carried them clear through a *potage croûte au pot,* and a *filet de sole Marguery* to a *poulet en casserole bordelaise* with absolute harmony—remains a diplomatic secret. Best of all, the whole thing was done with absolute secrecy and with no fear of that unfortunate "leakage" which spoils so many diplomatic conversations of the sort.

Suffice it to say that the press next morning carried the news that "following upon informal conversations held in Paris last night the impasse which existed in the Desert of Gobi in Inner Thibet is definitely lifted. No details are announced but it is understood that a formula was found which allows a *via media* on the basis of the Locarno agreement, the Balfour note, the Kellogg Pact, and the Binomial Theorem, each of the great powers consenting to stand in the light of a *particeps criminis*. Beyond that the public is not informed."

Anyway that will hold it.

II

The Brown-Jones Embroglio

Now wouldn't it be a funny thing if people's ordinary lives were run on diplomatic lines. Suppose, for example, that that row that went on intermit-

Man had not yet learned to shave.

We may picture the primitive man looking at his reflection in a pool of water: the idea of shaving dimly haunted his dawning intelligence.

Men began to break and chip flint stones in the attempt to make razors. Then came the discovery of how to make a razor out of iron by melting it and beating it flat. Civilization had begun and Athens arose with its beautiful barber shops.

Rome followed and shaving was carried to a higher pitch. Among the Greeks old superstitions had lingered and many philosophers had beards and the gods were depicted with long white beards. But the Roman gods were all clean shaven and had a neat snappy appearance.

Barbarian tribes overwhelmed Rome. The wonderful civilization was plunged into barbarism, or rather into unbarbarism. The Vandals, the Goths and the Berbers had no barbers. Civilization went backward and for long centuries men wore long whiskers. The crusades were fought to compel the eastern races to adopt beards.

Then came the revival of learning and the new age of science. Galileo invented the glass mirror which helped to introduce again the old belief in a clean shave. Leonardo da Vinci dreamed of a safety razor—called by him a Gilletta—and even left drawings of a barber's chair.

The discovery of the new world opened vast possibilities for barber shops in New York. The Negro brought from Africa was easily taught to black boots. The period of the industrial revolution followed. New inventions soon created the swivel chair, the spittoon and the revolving brush. The conquest of British India brought to Europe the Shampoo, a source of incalculable wealth. The eager rush to get shaved and to look all alike precipitated the French Revolution and plunged Europe in war. But the rise of Napoleon soon proved that the neat, clean-shaven French could outfight all the soldiers and outmarch— by their lack of weight. Only at sea the rough hairy tars of England still held their own. But the advent of steam, bringing with it the steam shampoo and above all the invention of the steamed towel, changed all that.

Rapid changes followed the path of science in the nineteenth century. The hollow ground razor first put the United States into the position of a great industrial power. Modern chemistry built up the Florida water industry while biology forged ahead with glycerine and cucumber and other products of the research laboratory. Clippers were invented by Faraday as far back as 1830, but it was only when the genius of Edison applied electric power to them that their use dominated the world.

The electrical age supplying light and power at

low cost revolutionized the entire world of shaving. Henceforth the economic problems of heating, lighting and decoration became uppermost. The nations entered on a fierce rivalry. France still excelled in lightness of touch, in the art of decorating the coiffure, England in the production of cheap soap, and Russia in her wealth of raw material. But in this as in everything, the United States won the palm by mass production and organization. The installations of the twenty-seat, ten-shine basement shop definitely left Europe in the rear; while the perfection of the safety razor removed much of the old-time industrial risk and cut insurance to a minimum.

Meantime, the emancipation of women threw open to them all the great avenues of life, including that of the manicuring profession in which they at once proved superior to the coloured races. These changes, however, led to a new equality and a freer intercourse of the sexes and manicuring undoubtedly weakened the marriage tie.

The intenseness of the struggle was too great. The consequence was the World War. It is impossible now to adjudge rightly the blame for it. We can see that the German military class had reached a perfection of clean shaving which made them eager to get on further. On the other hand, the desire of the French to recapture Lorraine, the home of the razor industry, was an element of unrest. The Prussians also, no longer content to see themselves as they were, wanted to break away from looking as they did and to get access to Florida Water, Witch Hazel, Bay Rum and civilization. The shaving off of the Manchu Pigtail plunged the east in a ferment. Only the Japanese, who had never grown beards, and the North American Indians, who couldn't, preserved a measure of control. The rest of the world plunged into Armageddon.

Only four years later was peace made, the negotiations being carried on at Versailles in the barber shop where President Wilson, Monsieur Clemenceau, Mr. Lloyd George and Orlando used to get their morning shave. Only there could the right atmosphere be found for united forbearance and waiting for one's turn.

Since the war, economic problems have absorbed the whole attention of the world. Prices rose and continued to rise and the cost of living assumed terrific proportions. By June in 1920 the cost of living was at its highest, a shave costing 35 cents, a haircut 75 cents, while Roman massage soared to the two dollar mark. This precipitated the crash of the stock exchange and the present depression.

Divided counsels prevail. If rigid economy is enforced and the great nations grow beards again, the whole barber business collapses; with it goes the razor business, bringing down iron and steel, the swivel chair business, causing a collapse in the furniture industry and the decline of forestry, together with Florida Water and Bay Rum impoverishing the State of Florida.

Others advocate an opposite course. What the world needs now is not less shaving but more, and, if need be, compulsory shaving. In the west there is widely advocated a farmer's pool, in which every farmer would have to take a bath and a shave every week. A huge loan to the Russians to let them set up Barber Shops on the Five Year Plan might save the world from Communism. In England the biggest men are shaving twice a day, but many classes are apathetic, living on the dole and not even washing. Meantime, in India, Mr. Gandhi's crusade against soap is said to be spreading an atmosphere of doubt.

In this perplexed world the average man will do well to hold to a middle course, shaving his face perhaps half way up, but not too near his ears.

But after all, history, even as specially written up in a "Barber's Outline," is no more peculiar than history as written up by each nation as a sort of advertisement of itself. One often wonders how the history of wars and victories would read if written up, not by our side (the only one we ever see) but by the other side. Here follow a few samples.

HOW NATIONS WRITE THEIR HISTORY

I

A Greek Account of the Battle of Salamis, B.C. 480

We knocked Hades out of the Persians.

A Persian Account of the Battle of Salamis, B.C. 480

We knocked Hell out of the Greeks.

II

Naval Victory of the Spanish Armada
(*As reported in the Spanish Associata Pressa of 1588*)

The Duke of Medina Sidonia returned yesterday with his fleet to the port of Seville after his triumphant campaign against England. The port was decorated with flags and all the shipping in the harbour bright with bunting and streamers, the Royal Banner of Spain alternating with the standards of Castile and Leon. King Philip, himself, received the Admiral on his landing from the state barge, and conferred upon him, as he knelt in homage, the order of the Spanish Chestnut, while a salute of a hundred guns greeted the conquering hero. The Duke's fleet is to some extent depleted, the losses due almost entirely to the tempestuous weather of their return voyage rather than to the futile attacks of their pusillanimous foes. But even heavier losses would be offset by the splendid triumph which thus frees the monarchy forever from the danger of the English pirates.

The Admiral reports that his fleet made an entire circuit of the British Islands, sweeping the enemy in front of them and then dragging them behind them. Nowhere did the enemy venture the hazard of a pitched battle but confined their attacks to hurried raids on the van of the fleet, all of which were easily beaten off.

The Admiral first came in contact with the English ships off the Port of Plymouth, where there was a considerable detachment of vessels under the command of the notorious pirate Francis the Drake and Johannis Hawkins, the slave dealer. From information received, it appeared that neither of these bandit leaders had much stomach for the fight. The Drake had to be dragged away from a game of bowls against a cowardly plea that he must finish the game. After beating off the Drake and Hawkins, the fleet swept up the Channel cleaning it of all enemies. It was decided not to capture London on this voyage, but to sweep the coasts of Scotia, or Caledonia, the northern portion of the British Isles still inhabited by savages.

Many of these savages were seen on the coast by our vessels and in many cases trade was opened with them in which it appears we lost heavily, an entire treasure ship being found missing.

The voyage home was uneventful. It is the opinion of the Admiral that the Western Island of the group, known as Erseland or Ireland, is splendidly situated for making trouble in all directions.

III

The Great Victory of Bannockburn
(*As Related by an Anglo-Norman Journalist in the Army of Edward II, A.D. 1314*)

The King's army was in contact today for four hours with the Scottish native levies. It has been decided not to fight them any more. They don't understand war.

Our army encountered the Scots, drawn up and extended in quite irregular fashion, entirely contrary to rules, along a small stream called by them "Bannockburn." As their word "burn" is taken to mean "stream," our geographical staff worked it out that Bannockburn means Bannock Stream, or Bannock River. This intelligence work showed us just where we were.

Our army, as it advanced, was led in the centre by the King in person, on the right by the Seneschal

Pilaffe de Volaille and on the left by the Justiciar
Fromage de Brie and accompanied by the entire array
of the greater Lords, including Fitz Urse of Urse,
and the Field Marechal Fitz Orse of Horse, and many
others of the last word in nobility.

We advanced with halbardiers and gonfaloniers in
front, with an attelage of four demi-culverins on
each flank. We had not covered our rear. We did not
think it necessary with rude opponents such as the
Scots.

The Scots were placed without any array or order,
being scattered among the coppices and ravines and
in the edges along the bogs—or, to use a more familiar word, the marécages—beside the river. Everything was contrary to the rules of war, even their
choice of the terrain, which was unfitted for knights
on horseback. For the most part we could not see the
Scots but we could hear everywhere along their lines
in the marsh and bush loud shouts of, "Hoot awa,
man!" "Here's to ye!" and "Just a wee Doc'k and
Dori's!" Here and there the cries seemed to break out
into a mournful chant in regard, it seemed, to Annie
Laurie, calculated to chill the spirits of all com-
batants.

The King decided to open the battle by sending
forward a fanfare of four trumpets and one haut-
boy. These had however barely taken up their station
when the Scots began to throw rocks and hit two of

the fanfares and struck the haut-boy just above his haut-de-chausses, knocking his wind out.

Our knights then charged in full array but found it impossible to attack the Scots owing to the impassable nature of the boggy ground into which their horses sank deep. It is feared that those who did not come back are there still. The Scots then set up a disorderly fight all along the line. It is very difficult to see them, and our archers found it almost impossible to get a fair shot at them. They wear a short costume called in their uncouth tongue a *kilt*, or more properly, a *demi-chemise*. When a Scot is moving very fast it is hard for an archer to know which is Scot and which is demi-chemise. To this is added a flying leather pouch called a *Sporan* and a sort of *Couvre-chef* or *Robe de nuit* called a *tartan*. Moreover the sword carried by the Scot, instead of being flat and straight (as under the Tournament Convention of Provence, Rule 10), is made with a curve in it, so that it is hard to tell where it is coming and where it is going. The Scots use it with no attempt at dexterity or skill. They just hit.

After three hours of fruitless attempt to reduce the engagement to something like rule and system, it was decided to abandon it as perfectly hopeless. The King ordered the Grand Marechal, Fitz Orse of Horse, to have a tucket sounded to indicate *laisser aller*. But it turned out to be unnecessary. Our trained army had anticipated it. In fact Fitz Orse himself had gone.

The rest of the array have drawn off hastily and we are now making full speed toward England. We have been compelled to abandon on the field the King's supply wagon containing ten casks of cognac from France. It has fallen into the hands of the Scots. They are not pursuing us. They seem to have lighted fires around the supply wagon and are singing something about Auld Lang Syne.

IV

The French Battle of Trafalgar
(*As Reported, Very Probably, in Napoleon's Morning Papers*)

Our Atlantic fleet under Admiral Villeneuve, which has been for some weeks scouring the ocean in search of the English fleet under Lord Nelson, at last got in contact with the enemy for a few hours yesterday, off Cape Trafalgar. Unfortunately, the oncoming of heavy weather prevented a decisive action and, the weather turning in the night to a violent storm, the English fleet was able to make off in the darkness. They had, however, suffered heavy losses in damage and in casualties, Lord Nelson himself being among the killed. Our ships did not escape without certain injury. One of them got quite a nasty crack under the stern and another lost the end of its bowsprit. Admiral Villeneuve on being interviewed said that he was sorry about Lord Nelson but these things will happen.

v

How the Dutch Won Waterloo
(Dispatch of Dutch General Staff, June, 1815)

NOTE: *We are apt to forget that the British Army only formed a minor part of Napoleon's enemies at Waterloo. Even leaving out the fifty or sixty thousand Prussians who turned up toward sundown, there were 45,000 Dutch and other Lowlanders, as beside only 25,000 British. Naturally the Dutch would think that they won the battle. Their accounts of Waterloo read, I am sure, very much as is below. I am not certain that I have the names of their generals quite straight, but they sound more or less accurate.*

As soon as it was known that Napoleon had left Elba it was realized that it would now be a straight fight between the French and the Dutch. Marshal Doppelbottel decided to wait for Napoleon and not to hurry him. This strategy proved effective. Napoleon turned up even sooner than we calculated, in the middle of June. Our men were not quite ready. The Schnapps had not yet come and only part of the gin and the cigars were not yet distributed. The result was that without us the English and the Prussians were badly beaten at Quatre Bras and at Ligny. Two days later Field Marshal Doppelbottel and his staff had things more or less in shape, though even then some of the men lacked parts of their equipment, having less than a pint of gin and for a good part of the day nothing to smoke. Having small faith in our English allies—under the Anglo-Indian Mynheer Wellington—it was decided to put them on the Waterloo hill with a wood behind them so that they couldn't run away, and tell them to stay there.

Leaving thus to Mynheer Wellington the mechanical or stationary part of the engagement, our men on the extreme right and on the extreme left were able to adopt highly mobile tactics, moving in circles so rapidly that the French couldn't get at them. Even Napoleon himself exclaimed in astonishment, "Why don't they stand still?" At one period of the battle Doppelbottel himself was eighteen miles away from Waterloo, eating lunch. The hard riding, coupled with the heat of the June sun, involved great fatigue, especially as very few of our troops had more than the opportunity for a light lunch, eaten in some cases without sitting down and without sleep after it. But the moment of triumph, when the French were slowly worn down by our mobile tactics and gave way in one vast rout, amply repaid our heroism. Nor should we forget the really meritorious part played by Mynheer Wellington and his British detachment. Our Field Marshal, compelled to leave them when he went away to lunch, found them at their posts and wide awake on his return. He generously says in his dispatches that their presence at Waterloo was a distinct and perceptible factor in this victory. Our generals on the day after the battle invited the British Staff in Brussels to an Old-fashioned Dutch Treat. It is understood that Holland will confer on Mynheer Wellington the Honorary Rank of a Schnappshalter.

VI

Brief Negro Summary of the Civil War
(*But this one is from O. Henry*)

"Yes, sir, I fought alongside de Ole Massa all fro' de war, till we had them Yankees licked and sent 'em back home."

VII

How the Portuguese Captured Vimy Ridge, 1917

Taken from a Portuguese work of about 1950, called *Guido ao Greato Warro entre Portugallo y Germania.*

(This I leave to the pen of some gifted veteran.)

PART V

Papers of the Ignoramus Club

At the time the Ignoramus Club was founded, great hopes were held as to the part it might play in a distressed world. These are reflected in the "papers" left behind after its untimely demise. The circumstances attending its organization and the general idea of its purpose are seen in the opening number of its journal. The part that it hoped to play in World Diplomacy is made evident in its second gathering. Its attempt to branch out into social welfare work is seen in the establishment of its summer camp for Overfed Boys. Unfortunately its career ended at the very moment when most might have been expected from it. Its members, being pledged to abstain from over-interest in anything and everything, began to feel that even the Club itself was too strenuous. Amazing though it may seem, its meetings came to a sudden end, and although the Club exists in a state of suspended animation, it has proved impossible—at any fixed date—to get together for the transaction of club business. It seems likely that the Club will take its place among the various defunct organizations, such as the League of Nations, the Anti-Mosquito Society, and the Concert of Europe, which lie strewn as wreckage along the path of human progress.

Its "papers" are here reproduced with no attempt to tone down the glowing optimism which first inspired them.

How We Organized

EVER since we started in our town our new Ignoramus Club, of which I'm the Secretary, I am stopped
on the street by people asking, "What is it? What is
it? How do I get in?" And letters! I'm simply bom-
barded by them—four yesterday and two more
today! As soon as it got 'round that there was no
fee, there was just a sort of stampede to get in when
we sat down at our Wednesday Luncheon meeting to
hear a talk on Abyssinia (it's out west in Canada; the
man had been there). I counted over a hundred
present, and more came in after the tickets were
taken up.

People get into the Ignoramus Club, you see, on
their brains, or at least on their minds, the kind of
minds they have. We do it by question and answer,
just by questioning the people who want to get in
and seeing if they have the right qualifications. For
example, yesterday after the Lunch we asked an ap-
plicant what was his idea of Mussolini; and he said
that he was pretty sure it was an artificial silk made
in Italy and used for lingerie!

He got in. That is exactly what the Club wants. You see it started from the idea that the world is all over-worried and preoccupied about peace and war, and nations who live God knows where, and economics and unemployment. People just grab for their paper in the morning to see who's in the Polish Corridor, and what's in the Saar Basin and whether the plebiscite among the Lat's will keep them Lat's or turn them into Slats.

It's too much. We think the world's going crazy. Our President, McSorley, put it that way. "Going crazy!" he said, just like that, snapping his fingers, "going crazy!" And McSorley's fine. It's silly about his ever having been in an asylum, because he wasn't. It wasn't an asylum at all, just a place! McSorley could have had the biggest law practice in town, but he was too versatile for it. He still has his office, and rows and rows of books in calf-skin. He sits there most of the day, working puzzles. So, of course, when we started the Ignoramus Club he was just the man for President.

Well, we have got together on the basis of complete ignorance of all this foolishness. We don't know where the Polish Corridor is and we don't care. Ask us where Manchukuo is and we just laugh! Just break out silly and laugh! You see, we don't know where it is and if you told us we'd forget it tomorrow and think it was somewhere else. In fact we are just like everybody used to be before the world went crazy.

At the last meeting somebody asked one of our lady members something about Flandin. Do we have ladies? Well, do we! What do you think we are, professors? Of course we have lady members, real peaches, and not one knows where Paraguay is, either, and they think that Chaco is chewing gum. Perhaps you saw in the papers the other day the story of how a man said to a girl at a dance, "I'd like to ask you for a dance but I must confess I'm just a little stiff from Polo," and she said, "Oh, that's all right, I don't care where you were born." Well, that girl is one of our members. She qualified on that remark.

What did the lady say about Flandin? Oh, she said that tablets like that were all right if you couldn't sleep.

As a matter of fact some of our members seem to get into the club just in time. They look sick and worn out when they come in, and in a week or two they quit worrying about the Polish Corridor, and they think the Belga is the name of a movie star and they're all right.

What do we do at the meetings? Come round some time and see. We have lunch meetings and evening meetings too; generally have a paper or a discussion, anything as long as the members don't know anything about it and don't care. We're having a lunch on Disarmament Wednesday. And of course in a way we're a "service" club. At least we're pledged to do something for the kiddies. We had a smoker for them, last time—you know, to raise money for the Scouts, great little fellows! But we lost out on it; the cigars cost too much. We had to borrow out of the little fellows' savings bank to get even. But we'll fix it all later. As McSorley said, "Boyhood is sacred." We'll see they get their money back. We can raise it from their parents. We're just starting up a Summer Camp for Underfed Kids. Some of us are going out next Saturday to see how the food is, and if there is fishing for the kiddies.

But come to any of the meetings and you'll see. The best thing we've started yet is our Legion of Humor. No, not honor, "Humor." It's a yellow ribbon the color of spilled egg; it goes on the lapel of the coat. Whenever any statesman or politician makes a special speech, the thing called a "vital pronouncement," we send it to him. But come round some time.

II

The Club Gives a Luncheon to Disarm Europe

You remember I told you, a little while back, about the Ignoramus Club of which I am the secretary and how the idea of the club is to get away from all the fuss and worry of the world, and not to know anything and not to care anything about it. You remember that I said we don't know where Czecho-slovakia is and we don't care. If I have spelt it right, I apologize. I didn't mean to.

We like to get away from all that and play golf, and go trout fishing and talk about back lot gardening and whether to tie tomatoes up on a stick or let them run on the ground. These are the real things in life. You get a few members of our club into a keen talk on tomatoes and you're hearing something.

But, of course, we like in a way to keep posted and we like to do good. And when the idea came up that if we held a lunch it might help to disarm Europe, the members were all for it. The proposal was that Dean Elderberry Foible, one of our senior members and a dean of the college here (palmistry, I think), should read a paper on disarmament and that would draw a good attendance especially if we had fresh asparagus and lots of it.

Our members will go further for fresh asparagus than anything else: Asparagus and cold salmon with a mayonnaise salad and with a clear soup in front of it, and after it one of those things—what do you call it, vol-o-vent?—anyway a German name. Some of the committee thought it too light, that the members would be too restless after it and wouldn't listen; a steak and kidney pie or cold lobster holds an audience down far better. They don't wake up much till the end.

So the upshot was that McSorley, the president, decided that we'd have the salmon and asparagus, with the steak and kidney pie on the side: It would boost the cost a little but he said he could make it up by using some of the money that the club had raised for the Children's Seaside Fund. It hadn't gone as yet, and we could make it up to the little tots, McSorley said, later on and in other ways, perhaps at Christmas. McSorley's crazy over children.

So we certainly had a fine turn-out. McSorley had to hit the bell three or four times before they would stop eating. Even while the dean was talking some of them were still reaching out for olives and things.

Dean Elderberry Foible makes a fine appearance. He has frosty white hair and a face as red and pink as an apple and a healthy look, not like a professor at all. The boys all say he looks distinguished. So he is. He writes letters to people like Mussolini and the queen of Moravians and Winslow Churchill. Mussolini answered one. I think it was Mussolini. Anyway someone did. It doesn't matter.

McSorley, when he announced that Dr. Foible would talk on disarmament, said he looked upon him as the finest classical scholar in America. But the dean very modestly said on rising that he must take exception to that; he was sure there must be at least 50 classical scholars in America as good as himself, or if 50 was an exaggeration, at any rate a dozen, or say six, or if not six at least two or three. He didn't know them but they might be there. Then he put on his glasses and took out a manuscript and began to read.

Our members don't like it when a speaker reads. They like it quick and snappy and with lots of local hits and byplays and some good side stuff about the ladies, or jokes like a hit at Charlie and Mary Prothers and everybody knows who it means though they're not named. So when the dean put his glasses on and began to read, there was a sort of sigh all round the luncheon room, and McSorley looked pretty restless.

Dr. Foible began by reading that the problem of disarmament went back to the Greeks and Romans and was one of the chief causes of the Philiponesian War, and that even before the Greeks some of the greatest wars of the old Babylonians were due to disarmament.

At that point McSorley rose and said he was sorry to interrupt the dean but he didn't think that the club wanted to go backward: he doubted whether any of the members knew where Babylon was, apart from those who had traveled in Central America. And he said that the Greeks and Romans seemed pretty far away too.

So Dean Elderberry Foible who is always very polite and old-fashioned said that perhaps it would be better if he were to drop right into the modern

world, and there was a murmur of pleasure and applause all around the room. The members all sat up
again and felt that they were going to get something.
So the dean began reading again.

"The modern world begins with the Black Death,
the expulsion of the Moors and the disruption of
feudalism."

There was a ripple of excitement at this because
they all thought he meant the Black Death was
coming, was going to happen now, and they thought
that the expulsion of the Moors was a good-natured
hit at the Sydney Moores' being put out of the Ar-
cadia Apartments after the last kid was born. But
when they gradually caught on that all these things
happened hundreds of years ago the members just
died on it again. So, of course, McSorley had to interrupt again and ask the dean to come right down to
the world of today.

So Dr. Foible gave a sigh and he turned over pages
and pages of his manuscript and he began again.

"The world of today—"

"That's the stuff," said McSorley.

"The   world   of   today   begins   with   Queen
Anne. . . ."

McSorley apologized and said that he was afraid
he must ask the dean to come right down to the
present. He said that it was such a glorious afternoon that he was sure the members would want to

get on to the links or into their back lot gardens and so he would ask the dean to talk about things of right now. He said members wanted to hear about the Europe of today and to contrast its quarrels and its angers and its brutal indifference to human suffering with the gentle peaceful temper of our people in America. McSorley hit the table and got quite angry about it.

Well, with that, late in the day as usual with professors, Dean Foible got well started. And it certainly was interesting! Did you know that right after the Great War all the European countries were joined in a League of Nations, so that there can't be any war anyway? Hence why disarm? The Dean made it as clear as anything, and the Ignoramus Club just ate it up. It seems that whenever any trouble starts the League holds a meeting at Lucarno, or at Stresa or at places like that, and that stops it.

Some of the members had a little trouble with the names because they didn't know, or didn't remember, that Lucarno is a big summer resort up on the Gatineau in Quebec. Stresa was worse, only McSorley interrupted and said he would ask Charlie Flint (Charlie's in the post-office) to tell the audience where Stresa is and Charlie answered right away that it is a post village of Hendrick County, Indiana, on the west fork of the White River, 30 miles northeast by north from Indianapolis. Some of the members thought he must have looked it up. Some thought he got it from his post-office business. Anyway he knew it.

Well, we gathered from the dean's talk that Europe is in a pretty ticklish condition, just the same. It seems to come and go. Last Tuesday things looked pretty good, and then on Wednesday, it appears, England held a "conversation" with Hitler or with someone and put things to the bad. However, it blew over till Friday and then someone "asked a question" in the French Chamber—the word means, "room, apartment, or bedroom"—and things started again.

The dean had just got to there when there was a big noise outside in the street and the fire engines went past. The audience could hardly sit. And then someone put his head in at the door and called out:

"Boys, it's Macpherson's flour and feed and they say one of the stenographers is caught in the upper office and she may get burnt up!"

So of course the meeting broke up and they all rushed for the street. To rescue the stenographer? Yes, of course, to rescue her if they could, and if not—well, they didn't want her to be burnt up, but if she was going to be burnt up anyway—you know what I mean—we're not Europeans, but if she had to be burnt up—well, you see it.

However, they got her out all except that her hair was pretty much scorched. Too bad, wasn't it?

Even so, I think the meeting left a sort of painful impression—all that talk of wars and quarrels. Most of the members, I think, were glad to get into their back garden lots and help the girls water the grass path. Glad we don't live in Europe, eh, what?

III

The Ignoramus Starts a Camp for Overfed Boys

By this time I suppose you all know pretty well all about the Ignoramus Club, of which I am secretary. Our lunch meetings, in connection with the disarming of Europe and things like that, have had a pretty wide reaction. We just started, as you know, with the idea that we were sick and tired of world trouble and wanted to laugh it off, but it almost begins to work the other way. Both the town papers gave our Disarmament Luncheon a big write-up, and when it got known that we were thinking of having a Symposium on the Gold Standard, the committee, so I hear, got a pretty broad hint to hold it off till the stock market is less touch-and-go than it is just now.

But anyway our Ignoramus Club is more than just a political club. There are plenty of things beside politics that you can know nothing about, if you're broad enough. We've a social club too, and already some of the leading girls, I mean the members' wives, like Mrs. Charlie Prothers, are beginning to talk about the idea of art sections.

But of course right from the start we are a service club, with the idea of doing good—doing good quietly and unassumingly, with plenty of publicity—you know the way it's done in all the best clubs now. So last Saturday we went out, a bunch of us, to look over the piece of ground we've leased beside Sunrise Lake as a Saturday Camp for Overfed Boys. It was McSorley, our president, who thought of that idea of the overfed boy as a starter. There had been some talk of underprivileged boys but a lot of us felt that we were not just sure whether boys are entitled to have privileges. Some of them are apt to take advantage of them. But, as McSorley said, you take an overfed boy and you've really got something that appeals. So the notion of our Club was that we'd get together a whole lot of these poor stuffed-up overfed little fellows, and get a Summer Camp for them, and send them out there every Saturday and train them down. We all got pretty enthusiastic and when we happened to hear of just the right piece of ground, about seven acres, right on Sunrise Lake, about twenty miles east of the town, everybody said get it right away. "Don't wait," says McSorley, "to look for the overfed boys. We'll find them later. Get the camp, put it in shape, try it out, and then there it is, all ready for these kiddies to go to." McSorley, when it comes to kids, has a big heart. In fact the notion of overfeeding a boy hit us all pretty hard.

Now this piece of land on Sunrise Lake, so we heard, was just the thing—a fine sandy beach and lots of big shade trees, and about three acres of open grass that could be marked off into a ball ground. You take an overfed boy and start him playing ball, eh? That's the stuff! That'll bring him down!

The financing of the idea was easy. All we had to do was to pay a certain amount in advance on the lease and then keep it as long as we liked. There was talk of calling for subscriptions but Dr. Elderberry Foible—the college dean I told you about, who is also the club treasurer—said that there was no need. He still had some of the money that we raised a month ago for the Girl Guides and that hadn't been used yet. He could take that. The Dean has a great head for money; some of the boys say he ought to have been in big finance.

All the place needed, it seemed, was a little clearing up of the ball ground to make it fit to play on. A few dollars would put that right. And then one of the club members, who's a minister, Reverend Quackenbush, struck the idea that some of us might go out ourselves and fix up the ball ground and then it wouldn't cost the Club a cent.

Reverend Quackenbush is a great fellow. He was the star pitcher on the ball team on two of the big theological colleges. He was on two because the first one put him out—not out of the ball team, but of the college. The other team went right after him when they heard he was free and gave him a free course and so his divinity cost nothing. He's a dandy fellow. You wouldn't know he was a minister at all. He smokes and swears just like the rest of the boys, no difference; and never talks about religion. But all the same he's minister of one of the biggest churches in town, and fills it every Sunday night. You ought to hear him talk, and thump the desk and just go for the congregation. I haven't, but they say he's great. He just tells those people straight out that they're going to hell. You ought to go some time.

Well, so it was fixed up that we'd go out to the camp ourselves and get it all fixed up for the overfed boys without any cost to the Club. We'd go in our own cars and take a lunch with us so that, if need be, we could work all day at the camp. To save money again it was arranged that the girls—I mean the members' wives—would put up lunch in baskets for us and then there would be nothing to charge to the Club funds except just the lager beer and cigars. Dr. Foible said he had the money for that all right. I think it was our Hospital Fund that still had something in it. Anyway he had it all right.

At first it was only just the committee who were going out to Sunrise Lake, and then a lot of the other members said they'd go too. A thing like that, you know, takes on, and this idea of the overfed boys has an appeal in it for any decent man, especially in the kind of weather it was that Saturday.

Well, we all drove out there to the camp and a wonderful day we had, I can tell you. Somehow when you do things like that for other people, without looking for anything for yourself, you get more pleasure out of it than if you were just looking for a good time. It was a great drive out there; certainly the country is at its best at this time of year and the roads simply A-1. We didn't start till comfortably after breakfast and took it easy, so the drive itself lasted about an hour. The place is just wonderful, with the little lake (it's only about three miles each way) like crystal glass, with a broad beach all sand and shingle and the big shade trees just back from it. Certainly when we get those poor little kids out there, they'll go wild over it.

Well, it turned out there was practically nothing to do to clear the ground up. It seems the farmer that owns the place had done that already. All we had to do was to mark out the ball ground, so that the overfed kids could play on it at any time. What was better still, it turned out Reverend Quackenbush had brought out a ball bat, and a ball and gloves and the whole outfit. He said you couldn't possibly lay out a ground right, and get it set properly to the light and everything, unless you tried it out first. So first thing we knew we picked up sides and we certainly had a great game, with all hands in it, including Dr. Foible. He said he couldn't run but Reverend Quackenbush told him he wouldn't have to, and sure enough he fanned him out each time he came to the bat. Reverend Quackenbush ran the whole game and certainly he knew how to do it. It is plain enough he's just wasted in the ministry.

So after the game some of the members lit fires to cook a beefsteak or two, and things like that. It's astonishing how men seem able to cook when they get out of doors—men right out of offices. Dean Foible said they were reverting to type, but I don't think so; they were just cooking. We had cold stuff too, cold meat pies and salads and berry pie. We'll have to go a little easy on overfed boys on that sort of stuff.

After we'd eaten all we could we just sat round and smoked—we couldn't move for a while—and someone said, "I wonder what Mussolini's doing now," and we had a laugh on that. Then somebody else said, "I wonder if the Zazis are going to make war on the Czecks," and that started another big laugh; because, you remember, that's the way our Ignoramus Club got started, not knowing and not caring about all that Europe tripe.

So we loafed round all the afternoon. Before we drove home, we arranged that some of the members will come out every Saturday. We may put a care-taker on the place (Dr. Foible says there's money still in our Mothers Day Endowment that would just pay for him), and he could help get the place ready for the overfed boys. Meantime we are all going to look round and pick up these overfed kiddies here and there and give them a big time. There's one little fellow I've noticed on a back street near my house so fat he can hardly walk. That seems to be just the class of kiddy we'd want to bring.

Meantime if you know of any, let us hear of them. If you know of any nice little fellows from what you'd call good families, pretty well off, and overfed, remember that the camp is organized and run for them—primarily. But come out yourself some Saturday anyway.

PART VI

Drama Section

It has always seemed to me that some of the good old Children's Fairy Stories could be revised in such a way as to fit them for this changing age. The attempt is here made to reproduce in dramatic form two old favorites as Red Riding Hood Up-To-Date *and* Beauty and the Boss. *Anybody bold enough to act them as drawing room pieces is welcome to. I suggest as other similar topics,* The Sleeping Beauty in the Wood Alcohol, Jack and the Bean Head, The Old Woman Who Lived in the Soo, Puss in Booze, *etc., etc.*

RED RIDING HOOD UP-TO-DATE

An Old-Fashioned Children's Story
as
A Play for New-Fashioned Children

CASTED CHARACTERS
(*As they appear*)

JANE ....*A maid*
MRS. HOOD ....*Mother of Red Riding Hood*
MISS RIDING HOOD....*Otherwise Red Riding Hood*
GAFFER GAMMON ....*A woodcutter of the period*
of whiskers
LORD WOLF ....*Son and Heir of the Marquis*
of Snarl
DOWAGER LADYHOOD..*Grandmother, à la mode*
CLARISSA ....*Her maid*

SCENE 1: *Mrs. Hood's Drawing Room*

Curtain rises to find:—

JANE (*A maid. She is moving about the room picking up odd things left around on the sofa and chairs—music, etc.*)—Dear me! What Miss Riding does throw about!—every time that young Lord Wolf telephones her to go out, she gets all in a flutter,

and just drops everything! Look at it— Music!—
Needles!—Work!! Goodness, that's my lady's step.

(*Enter* Mrs. Hood.)

Mrs. H.—Where is Miss Riding?

Jane—Gone up to her boudoir, I think, ma'am.

Mrs. H.—Please ask her to come here.

Jane—Yes, ma'am!

(*Exit* Jane.)

Mrs. H.—Dear me! (*Sinking languidly into a
chair.*) It is *so* hard to look after these young girls.

(*Enter* Riding Hood *dressed to go out.*)

R. R.—What is it, Mamma?

Mrs. H.—Only to see what you are doing. Why
are you dressed to go out?

R. R.—I thought of—of going—of going (*evidently making an excuse*) to—to see Grandmamma.
(*Telephone rings.* Riding *answers. Slyly.*) Yes—yes
—I'm just ready. No—I can't— All right then, in
the little wood. (*Rings off.*)

Mrs. H. (*Severely.*)—Who was that, child?

R. R.—Lord Wolf, Mamma.

Mrs. H.—And did I hear you say you would meet
him again?

R. R.—Why not, Mamma?

Mrs. H.—Because Lord Wolf is a dangerous young
man and he hasn't a penny. His father, Old Lord
Wolf, has cut him out without a penny.

R. R.—Oh, Mamma! How dreadful!

Mrs. H.—So be careful. Now, if you are going to your grandmother's, take her this pâté de foies gras, and these champignons aux truffles and this pint of Pommery.

R. R.—All right, Mamma—and if I meet Lord Wolf (*with a little bow*) I'll be very careful.

CURTAIN

Scene 2: *A Forest* (*of drawing room ferns, rubber trees and flowers*)

(*Enter* R. R. *singing and picking flowers.*)

R. R. (*Sings*)—

> Les fraises et les framboises,
> Les vins que nous avons bus
> Et les belles villageoises
> Nous ne les verrons plus.

> J'ai rencontré Françoise,
> Je lui ai dit, ma mie
> Montre-moi tes framboises,
> Montre tes fraises aussi.

> Les fraises et les framboises . . . etc.

(*Enter* Old Gaffer Gammon *very bucolic, with white whiskers à la Longfellow.*)

G. G.—Good morning, missie.

R. R.—Good morning, Gaffer.

G. G.—Ha' ye seen young master hereabouts?

R. R.—No, Gaffer.

G. G.—T'owd Lord sent me wi' a message for un and a' can't find un.

R. R.—A message?

G. G.—Ay! A letter like.

R. R.—Let me see it.

G. G.—Naw. I got un here but a' said a' maun show un to nobody.

(Exit G. G.)

R. R.—I wonder what Lord Wolf's father—it seems strange— Oh! Good morning.

(Enter YOUNG LORD WOLF *in golfing costume, very gay and debonair.)*

LORD W.—I say! How jolly meeting you here, what?

R. R.—I'm really just here by accident. I'm only going over to Grandmamma's.

LORD W.—So am I, by accident. I'm just going across to have a smack on the links. I say, what's in the basket. *(Tries to take the basket.)*

R. R.—Please don't. It's for Grandmamma.

LORD W.—Oh! Law! Pâté de foie gras! Come on!

R. R.—No, you mustn't.

LORD W.—Come on! Here's a spoon. Let's open it up.

R. R.—No!—No! (*Struggle.*) (*Angrily.*)—No, I won't stay any longer.

Lord W.—Yes, yes, *DO* stay! In fact you've got to stay. There's something, Riding, I want ever so much to say to you. (*Takes her hand.*)

R. R.—You mustn't.

Lord W.—Yes, I will, Riding, ever since I've seen you, I've loved you more every day.

R. R.—Oh, Lord Wolf—Arthur— You really mustn't—and anyway Mother says— Oh, I can't tell you what she says—but I simply *mustn't* love you. (*Breaks away and runs.*)

Lord W. (*In agonized voice*)—Riding, Riding, come back!

CURTAIN

Scene 3: *Dowager Lady Hood's Drawing Room in Hood Towers*

D. L. H. (*Languidly making up before a glass. Very fashionable and La-de-da—aged 46 or so.*) (*A tap on the door.*)—Yes, come in!

(*Enter* Maid.)

Maid—Miss Riding is here, ma'am. Shall I show her in?

D. L. H.—Yes, please, Clarissa.

(*Enter* Riding Hood.)

R. R.—Good morning, Grandmamma.

D. L. H.—Good morning, my child.

R. R.—I've brought you some pâté de foies gras and some champignons aux truffles and a pint of Pomméry that Mother sent.

D. L. H.—Thanks, so much. Put them down on the table, dear. (R. R. *puts baskets on the table, then goes over to her grandmother.*)

R. R.—Oh, Grandmamma, how large your eyes look!

D. L. H.—Yes, dear, it's a new eye wash—rather effective, isn't it?

R. R.— —and, Grandmamma, how long your ears look!

D. L. H.—It's these pendent earrings, darling. I'm a little old-fashioned about them.

R. R.— —and, Grandmamma, how bright your nails look!

D. L. H.—A new French nail polish—quite chic, don't you think, child?

R. R.— —and, Grandmamma, how red your lips look!

D. L. H.—It's my new tangée from Paris—(*Row and clatter outside. Voice of* LORD WOLF—)

LORD W. (*From without.*)—I say I will go in.— Let me in, I say (etc., etc.)

MAID (*From without.*)—No, you mustn't, Lord Wolf.

(WOLF *bursts in impetuously.*)

Lord W.—I say, Lady Hood, what's all this tommyrot I've been hearing—

D. L. H. (*Coldly.*)—What do you mean?

Lord W.—About not allowing Riding to speak to me—I won't stand it!

D. L. H.—You forget yourself, Lord Wolf.

Lord W. (*Angrily.*)—I tell you I mean to marry Riding. I don't care what you or anybody—

D. L. H. (*Coldly.*)—Lord Wolf, I shall never allow my granddaughter to marry a penniless young man, disinherited by his father.

Lord W.—Oh, so that's it, is it—? (*Just then more noise at the door.*)

(*Enter* Mrs. Hood *and* Gammon.)

Mrs. H.—I got rather anxious about Riding. I followed her over and just at your door I met this old man who seems to have a letter for Lord Wolf. I told him to give it to me to read but—

G. G.—Na! Na! only for the young master himself.

Lord W.—Well, here I am, Gammon. Hand it over. (*Takes letter.*) Ah—from the Governor. Let's see what the old boy has to say. (Lord W. *reads.*)

"Just learned of malicious stories being circulated to the effect that I had disinherited you. Can not understand how such a miserable lie was started. Believe me, my dear Arthur, you have my entire confidence, and, in point of it, I am settling £500,000 and Wolf Castle on you at once.

Your loving
FATHER."

(*Whistling.*)—I say! pretty generous of the old boy, what?

D. L. H. }
MRS. H. } —Oh!

MRS. H.—Arthur! What wonderful news. Riding, don't hang back like that, come and congratulate dear Arthur.

R. R. (*Arms open.*)—Arthur.

LORD W. (*Advancing.*)—Riding.

CURTAIN

BEAUTY AND THE BOSS

or

The Sacrifice of a Stenographer

CHARACTERS

(As they appear)

WILLIE NUT .... *An Office Boy*

PHOEBE SIMP .... *An Outgoing Stenographer*

MISS CUTIE BEAUTY OF BUTTE,
  MONTANA .... *An Incoming Stenographer*

MR. JOHN JACKAL......... *A Brute Who Eats Stenographers*

MUG BILL .... *The Office Janitor*

THE PAW OF BEAUTY OF BUTTE *Straight from Montana with a Gun*

BEVY OF STENOGRAPHINETTES *Applying to Be Stenographers*

SCENE: *A New York Business Office*

The Curtain rises to find WILLIE NUT *and* PHOEBE SIMP *moving about.* PHOEBE *has her out-*

of-door things on, and is snivelling as she moves around the room, packing up her things into a valise. There is a door at the side marked "PRIVATE."

WILLIE—Don't take it so hard, Miss Phoebe.

PHOEBE—Take it hard— Well, I guess— Think of all I've stood for a month already—and now he's fired me! Look at that (*showing her wrist*), he done that, see! grabbed me by the wrist and, "Take this dictation," says he— "You brute!"—says I—then he hit my ear—look at that—bo—oo—oo.

WILLIE—Oh! Miss Phoebe! (*He picks up the poker that lies near the grate and shakes it at the door marked* PRIVATE.) Sometimes I just feel as if I'd like to go right into that man in there and KILL him! (*Roars and noise from inner room.*) "Ha-ar! Ya-ar! Isn't that girl gone yet?" (*Crawls and puts down the poker. Then in a meek voice.*)—She is just going, Mr. Jackal. (*Noises and growls subsiding. Nine strikes, very audibly and distinctly from a clock in the centre on the wall: One! Two! Three! Four! Five! Six! Seven! Eight! Nine! A knock.* MUG BILL *opens the door.*)

MUG BILL—A young lady to see Mr. Jackal.

(*Enters—a timid little stenographer neat as a Puritan.*)

THE STEN.—Is there a place advertised here for a stenographer?

PHOEBE (*Still sobbing.*) —Yes, sit down. He's in there.

MUG BILL (*Putting his head in again.*) —Two more!

> (*Enter—two more little stenographers looking just like the first.*)

BOTH TOGETHER—Is there a position—

PHOEBE (*Still sobbing.*) —Yes—there is—a degrading position—if you want it—sit there, girls—he's in there.

MUG BILL—Three more!

> (*Enter—three more stenographers as before.*)

THE THREE ALL TOGETHER—Is there a position—

PHOEBE—Yes, there is—sit down, girls—right there—wait, I'll just let him know. (PHOEBE *goes and knocks timidly at the door marked* PRIVATE.)

VOICE WITHIN—Eh! What! Gr-r-r!

PHOEBE—The girls is here, Mr. Jackal.

VOICE—Ha-a-a-r! (*The door opens. Enter* MR. JACKAL. *He has a mask like a hog. He stands and looks.*) Har! Har! Gr-r! Are you the new stenographers?

ALL THE GIRLS TOGETHER—Yes, sir.

MR. JACKAL—Then you *don't suit!* Zar! Gr-r! Get out!! (*He waves his arm at the stenographers, who all leap to their feet and rush out of the door.* MR. JACKAL *re-enters his private room and slams the door. A knock at the door.*)

PHOEBE—Come in.

(*Enters*—MISS CUTIE BEAUTY OF BUTTE, MON-
TANA—*street clothes—reticule—vanity case—
speaking in what is considered, in Butte, Montana, a highly cultivated tone, but simpering.*)

MISS CUTIE—Oh! say, folks, is this here Mr.
Jackal's office? Tee, hee!

PHOEBE (*Half sobbing.*)—Yes—I suppose you're
the new stenographer.

CUTIE—Yes—that is, we don't call it that no
more in Montana—I'm an amanuensis—tee, hee!

WILLIE—A man—which?

CUTIE (*Bridling.*)—Amanuensis—it means a gentleman's Vademecum—

PHOEBE—Say, did you come all the way from
Montana looking for this job?

CUTIE—A-ha— A well, not altogether—let me tell
you how it was— (*They gather in a confidential
group.*) You see, out there in Butte, I had a gentleman friend—ED. GOPHER—Eddie, they all called
him—and this gentleman—he used to take me out
to church Sundays, a-ha— (*All three wriggle and
wiggle.*) And he took me pictures, nights and walks
days—tee—hee! Well, so he says, one night, he says
—"Cutie," says he, "how about getting married?"
Tee-hee! Well, I was just kind of girlish about it—
a-ha! and I just picked up a banana skin and I gave
him a swat over the face—just girlish—but it kind

of scared him—he run off and beat it out of town.

OTHERS—My! Oh, say! My!

CUTIE—Ye-es! I went home and told Paw—Paw loaded up his shotgun—say, Paw looked for Eddie all around town for six days.

OTHERS—Well, say!

CUTIE—But he didn't get him!

THEM—Well, now!

CUTIE—Then Paw heard Eddie had gone to New York— So we came right along— Paw's around town somewhere with his shotgun right now.— (*Noise from within, gr-r! zar-r!*)

WILLIE—Just leaving, sir, just leaving.

MUG BILL (*Shows his head in at the door.*) — That taxi's waiting.

WILLIE—I'm going with Miss Phoebe, I'll help you with your things.

> (*Exit* MUG BILL *and* WILLIE, PHOEBE *with valises.* CUTIE *takes off her things and moves about, examines the room. Bell buzzer sounds on the wall.*)

CUTIE—Say, ain't that a cute little bell! I wonder what that's for? Hr-r! (*Shouts from within.*) Why don't you answer? (*Door opens—there appears* MR. JACKAL. *He stands staring at* CUTIE.)

MR. JACKAL—Who are you? What! Eh! Don't answer! Speak! Gurrr!

CUTIE—I am the new amanuensis. Tee-hee! They

sent me from the agency! Say, I think this office is real cute, eh! Tee-hee!

MR. JACKAL—SIT DOWN!

CUTIE—Don't you talk in that tone to me! I ain't used to taking no freshness from gentlemen.

MR. JACKAL—SIT DOWN!

CUTIE (*Sits down and adjusts herself in front of a typewriter.*)—If I sit down it's because I want to sit down, see! I ain't sitting down because you told me to sit down—

MR. JACKAL—Take this dictation from me!

CUTIE (*Leaping up.*)—I don't take no dictation from no man— (*Seizing poker.*) You offer to dictate to me and I'll brain you— (*There is a pause—both remain looking at one another.*)

CUTIE—And anyway I can't work one of them machines—

MR. JACKAL (*Impatiently.*)—All right! All right! I can see to that myself after lunch.

CUTIE—Cut that right out now. Don't you start asking me to lunch!

MR. JACKAL—I didn't!

CUTIE (*Sneeringly.*)—Just as well—and anyway all I can take for lunch is just nothing, just a little steak, a little fricasseed chickens or a lobster.

MR. JACKAL—All right, very good. Now take your book; write shorthand. Can you take anything right off fast?

CUTIE—Take anything off! (*Rising in indignation.*) I'll let you know I am not the kind of girl you think, I am the kind of girl . . .

MR. JACKAL—There—stop— If you can't use a typewriter and you can't write shorthand, what are you here for?

CUTIE—Don't you start implying anything like that. I know you. I met them girls on the stairs. Say, Mr. Jackal, you just ought to be ashamed of yourself. (JACKAL *goes and leans his elbow on the mantelpiece, head in hand, then, in a deep, hollow, humbled voice*—)

MR. JACKAL—Tell me, little girl—whence come you?

CUTIE—Whence I come from where?

MR. JACKAL—Ay, whence?

CUTIE—I'm from Montana.

MR. JACKAL—Ay, from Montana! (*In a tragic tone.*) Where the men are men and the women— tell me it is so, is it not—the women are women! (*Half sobs.*)

CUTIE (*Deeply moved.*)—Yes, from Montana where the men are real men, like my Eddie! You don't know Eddie, do you? Eddie Gopher. I'm looking for him anywhere.

MR. JACKAL (*With great meaning.*)—Ha! Looking for your Eddie.

CUTIE—Yes, me and Paw! Paw's out on the street

right now looking for him.

Mug Bill (*Head in door.*)—There is a party here asking to get in.

Mr. Jackal—A party? How many—

Mug Bill—Just one.

Mr. Jackal—Of how many?

Mug Bill—None, didn't I say—

Voice—Hold on, young man. I'll *go* in.

> (*Enters the* Paw of Beauty of Butte—*leggings—long hair—moccasins—long gun 7 feet long—looks like Montana.*)

Cutie—Paw!—!

Paw—Cutie!—! What's all this? Has this man been insulting you? If he has, by Jehoshaphat— (*Getting his gun ready.*)

Cutie—No, no, Paw, he ain't . . .

Paw—You ain't! (*Grounds the gun and looks around.*) But what is this! you've been alone with her, alone with my little gal, in one of them New York offices; that's enough! By jumping Jehoshaphat! (*Gets his gun ready again.*)

Cutie—Paw—behave!

Paw—Stand back, Darter! You don't understand these things. If this man's insulted yer, why, I got to kill him!! Else, how can I face our Eddie when I find him and tell him to marry you.

Cutie—Paw! Paw! (*Trying to throw herself in his way.*) Paw, don't! I ain't only seen him ten min-

utes—and, Paw, I love him—I don't want Eddie now
—I love him, this man here—this here man! Paw!
Paw!

Paw (*Solemnly.*)—I can't help it, little darter.
He's got to die. (*Calling.*) BILL!

(*Enters* Mug Bill.)

Paw—I got to kill this man. See! Out in Montana,
we don't kill a man in secret; we do it in the open.
Fetch me some witnesses.

Mug Bill—All right, they ain't gone away yet.
(*Calling out of the door.*) Girls! Willie! Phoebe!

(*Enter the stenographers and* Willie *and*
Phoebe.)

Mr. Jackal (*Up to this time he has not spoken;
he has assumed an upright position, very erect at the
far side of the room.*)—You're right. Shoot me! But
let me ask for one thing. Are you an expert marksman?

Paw (*Getting out his powder horn and touching
up the priming.*)—Marksman! By heck, I can hit a
squirrel at 200 yards on the hop. I mind the day when
me and Lem Smith—

Mr. Jackal—Very good. Then shoot straight—
put the bullet here—exactly the top my forehead.
(*He indicates the spot. Cries of horror,* OH! OH!
from all the girls.)

Paw—All right, boss, all right! Get set! Now
then, girls, you all say one! two! three! and then

when you say three I'll shoot. . . . Are you all set? Now!

CHORUS—ONE! TWO! THREE!

BANG!!!!!!!

(*The mask falls, revealing the true face of* MR. JACKAL.)

CUTIE—Eddie! Eddie! It's my Eddie! Disguised!

EDDIE—Disguised, yes! But only as a means of bringing you to me. By this article of advertising for a stenographer in New York, I was bound to find you again.

PAW—Har! Har! Har! I get it—darned good. Now then, girls, One, Two, Three! (*On the three* EDDIE and CUTIE *rush into one another's arms.*)

CURTAIN

Personalia

LOOKING BACK ON COLLEGE

DURING all my thirty-five years of college teaching I always felt that there was no profession in the world for which I would have exchanged my own. I have never had any envy of business men, no matter how rich, who work all the week and all the year, no matter how easy and simple their work may be as compared with Greek verbs and simultaneous equations.

College teachers enjoy a spacious feeling toward the flight of time that no business man can know. They have time to *think*. Very often they *don't* think but at least they have time to. Their fixed engagements are few, their open time—they don't like to call it a *vacation:* they resent that—is vast and alluring as an empty wood. In a well-ordered college—its finances unchangeable, its trustees mute as ancestral portraits, its departments feudalized into little kingdoms, with nothing of the bossy and brutal interference from above that begins to disfigure so many colleges—a professor's life in its outlook touches as close to eternity as any form of existence still with us. In the past there was the mediaeval scriptorium, with a stained-glass window under the light of which a scholar copied upon vellum a volume of Polybius: or there was, shall we say, an Elizabethan rectory where a pious Hooker penning his *Ecclesiastical Polity* looked out over the clipped lawns and the immemorial trees, and beyond that to the distant sea, and the clouds and the sunset. This timeless age our hurrying world destroyed. The professor still keeps a little bit of it: and it elevates his life to a plane that outsiders never can know—fortunately, or they would scramble for our places.

I am not decrying outside work. It is necessary. The world cannot go on without it. But we do not realize its artificial and unnatural character. Our race has been schooled by long ages of compulsion, tied to our tasks like galley slaves, till we have been bred and evoluted to the "work-habit" and take it now for granted. We are surprised when we see a real man— like a Portuguese West African—who won't work. We do not understand that what the business man does, except that it is necessary, is quite inexplicable. We can understand a man hunting deer, or fishing, or playing golf or chess—these are real things. But why should a man spend his busy days in trying to sell things—which he hasn't got—and make things which he never sees? At times he get absorbed in it— and it becomes self-explanatory. But mostly it is just for the reward, the money and things it will buy. Partly, too, animal habit.

But with the professor it is all different. He has
no *work* in that sense, not if he is a real professor.
His class?—you can't keep him out of it. Preparing
his lectures?—that's no more work than a lion getting up his appetite. People who do not live in colleges cannot understand the unworldly absorption of
the professor's task. Poets talk of the joy of the
springtime—of the month of May breaking the hills
into green and filling all the air with rapture. The
"merry month of May," says the poet. I know a
merrier. Give me the murky month of February,
with the snow blowing on the window pane of the
class-room, the early darkness falling already and the
gas-light bright in the class-room; that and a black-
board, and a theorem, and a professor—the right
kind, absorbed, ecstatic, and a little silly. Give me
that and the month of May may keep its fronds and
toadstools as it will.

.   .   .   .

One would imagine that anyone who looks back,
as I do, over nearly fifty years of college life, would
know a great deal about the problems of education.
Indeed I made a remark to that effect at a banquet
given to me by my past students in exultation over
my leaving McGill. I said, I think, that the setting
sun, breaking out from under the clouds that had
obscured the day, illuminated the landscape with a
wider and softer light than that of noontide. But that

was just oratory, or gratitude for a good dinner. As a matter of fact the great problems of education seem to be just about as unsolved now as they were half a century ago.

When I entered college there was much talk of co-education, half a dozen dangerous-looking girls having just slipped into the classes. The question was, would women ruin college education, or would they endow it with newer, nobler and higher life? or, more simply, were they a curse or a blessing, a nuisance or a charm? I still don't know. You can argue it either way according to how you are feeling. Certainly college is not what it was; but neither is anything. Old people live, and always have, in a world hurrying to ruin, young people in a world bright with the colours of the morning.

We talked, too, of the classics, very much to the fore fifty years ago, but even then having to bear the first onslaught of the rival studies of science and commerce. It was asked whether the study of the classics was the only real approach to the higher cultivation of the mind or whether they were a mere historical survival, a remnant of a rude, illiterate but reviving age, when any book in Latin seemed a treasure, and any play in Greek a masterpiece. Are the classics really great literature? I don't know. They don't sound like it, but that may be my fault. Can a man really be a gentleman without studying the Greek moods and tenses; perhaps he can, but can he be the best kind of a gentleman? I don't know. Greek has been pushed overboard by the sheer pressure of the crowd on deck. Is it a loss? I don't know.

And what about science? Is a person as totally ignorant of chemistry as I am, as almost totally ignorant of physics, biology, geology as I am, any the worse for it? He must be. And yet if you do learn by heart, and then forget, the names of the palaeozoic, mesozoic, and kainozoic ages, are you any better off than the Greek student who knows what they are anyway and can't forget it. Is a smattering of *science* anything more than a list of words; or does it unlock for us the vast general store-house of the world's wisdom on which alone a reasonable outlook can be based? I think so. Which? Both.

Then, as to method of education. I hear students nowadays say that *lectures* are no good, that you don't learn anything by hearing a professor read out notes. We used to say that, too, fifty years ago. It is claimed now that you can get it all out of a book. So it was then. So you can. But will you? The student's mind, so it is said, must work for itself, assimilate its own material; so it must, of course, but how do you do it? Plato and Aristotle were giving lectures 2000 years ago: and men very like them will be giving lectures, the same lectures, 2000 years from now. Only people who have had to study for themselves, as I had to, know how good lectures are, even the worst of them—how hard it is to work without set times and hours and set companionship. Let the lecturers keep on lecturing, and if some of the lectures are worthless, the rest will seem all the snappier. After all it is not the *words* that the teacher reads or recites or quotes; it's the teacher himself—the peculiar element of personal magnetism or whatever one calls it—that "gets over" to the class.

So it would seem that the college is always new and yet always old: living its own life on its own vital energy. The problems of education are just the shifting of the sunlight on the surface of a moving current.

THE END OF THE SENILITY GANG

An Episode at McGill University

As a general rule nothing is in worse taste than to put personal or local matter in a book meant for the public. But this little volume of *Funny Pieces* covers such a queer scope and claims so much of its readers' indulgence, that there is no harm in making it a little queerer and its claims a little more exacting.

After I had been teaching at McGill University for thirty-five years the Governors of the institution, in a sudden passion of righteous anger against old men, turned out to grass the thirteen of us who had reached the age of sixty-five. In a sense, the joke of this is decidedly on me. Very often in my writings of past years I had expressed my doubts of the capacities of old men. I had once even fervently written:—

"Is it true that men succeed when they are young by the force of their mind and the power of their body, and later on in their old age encumber the offices of honour and emolument, monopolize, through the prestige of what once was theirs, the pages of the press and the foreground of the drama, the dead ashes of extinct genius choking the living fires below? Is the world being 'ruined' by 'venerable' statesmen, wars lost by 'veteran' generals, and spiritual life numbed by 'venerable' prelates?"

. . . .

Perhaps I should have added, ". . . and students put to sleep by 'revered' professors?"

. . . .

In the light of this it might be thought that my being retired recalled the amusing situation chronicled in the Bible (*Book of Kings*), and made amusing by the queer way in which in our Bible italics are used for words not actually in the original Greek or Hebrew. The text is:—

"And he said, 'Saddle me the ass.' And they saddled *him*."

. . . .

At any rate, when my students learned that my time had come, they held a dinner in my honour in connection with the final meeting of the session of the Political Economy Club. In order not to let ourselves be carried away by the sentiments and speeches of such an occasion, we adjourned after dinner to the meeting place of the Political Economy Club where we listened to papers on the Gold Standard. I do not know of anything which can better reconcile a man to laying down the work he has done for thirty-five years than listening to papers on the gold standard. . . . Next day I wrote up the occasion for the local press in the form that follows:—

END OF SENILITY GANG AT MC GILL

College Malefactor Goes to Lethal Chair

The first execution of a member of the "senility gang," which has terrorized McGill University for years, took place last night with the removal of the malefactor Leacock, alias Steve, who was sent to the lethal chair, according to the sentence, by the Political Economy Club. Before the execution the condemned man ate a hearty meal and at his own request was served with a strong draught of spirits. At his own request, also, he was served with a second, but a third was refused.

Before the fatal procession was formed the Rev. Dr. Pick (Alfred Pick, chairman of the meeting) led in prayer, and read from the gospel according to John Stuart Mill, Chapter III, verses 1-17 on "The Final Adjustment of Value."

The condemned man was asked if he had anything to say and said a few words in a firm, manly voice. He said he regretted nothing he had done and that if he had 35 more years to live, he would do it over again. The suggestion that he might live for 35 years more was received with visible emotion by those present, especially Dr. Hemmeon, who succeeds to his chair.

The procession was then formed, the Rev. Dr.

Pick leading and intoning as the procession moved the words of the Political Economy Club hymn, "Abide with me, fast falls the index number." Arrived at the place of execution the prisoner was placed in the lethal chair of the Political Club and Mr. Ronald Leathem proceeded to read to him his paper on the Gold Standard in its Mathematical Aspect. The prisoner was pronounced unconscious in five minutes, a fact of interest in the present discussions in regard to the removal of criminals.

It will be recalled that this is the first of the executions that follow on the conviction of the notorious "Senility Gang," and the sentences of Chief Justice Sir Edward Beatty of last autumn. The gang, made up of 13 members, apart from the man Brodie Brockwell, now under reprieve, and several others known to the police but still at large, had led in the sudden and criminal outbreak of senility, of which McGill University was made the centre.

The next execution will be that of Martin, known to the underworld as "Charlie the Dean," and said to have a medical degree and to have been in the same class—in fact to be in the same class—as the notorious Dr. Neill Cream, or Jack the Ripper. The Chief Justice, Sir Edward Beatty, in passing sentence, said it was immaterial whether Martin was, or was not, Jack the Ripper. The essential thing was that his execution will help to put a stop to medicine at Mc-

Gill, which was all he cared for. Martin, it appears, was accused of medicine by Hans Oertel (a Dutch employee), whose suspicions of Martin had been aroused by finding a grey hair underneath his billiard table.

But there is a widespread feeling outside the walls in his favour, and there is even an organized attempt on the part of outside crooks to prevent his execution. It is said, however, that Martin can expect no clemency from any appeal to the Crown, it being understood that His Excellency Lord Tweedsmuir strongly favours his execution as opening up a position for one more Scotchman in Canada.

After "Dean Charlie," comes, probably, the removal of the patriarch of the gang, Hermann Walter, whose conviction for senility rested on reliable evidence that he put on a German play in the vernacular as the first and only one in Canada. The defence plea that it was not really German broke down under evidence that a number of the persons in the audience recognized German words and even poetic phrases, such as "ein glas Bier," "hier ist eine Cigarre," etc., etc. Old Walter seems childishly unconscious of his fate, sings and swears to himself in German and gives lectures on William Goethe, unaware that Goethe is dead.

Very little sympathy is felt for Stansfield—known in criminal circles as "Melting Pot Joe"—who goes next after Walter. The peculiar atrociousness of his crime (he is convicted of Metallurgy) puts him out of consideration. At the same time as, or shortly after "Melting Pot Joe," the Frenchman Villard, alias Paul, alias "Mooshoo," will meet his fate. He stands convicted of wearing the Legion of Honour and taking part openly in the Communist group called the *Alliance Française*.

The criminal still under reprieve, Brockwell, otherwise "Deuteronomy Brock," is said to be devotely preparing himself to meet his end. He spends his time solely in reading the Hebrew scriptures, especially to see what it says about Hell and whether the governors will go there.

With the execution of the remaining criminals, McGill University will be rid in time of the outbreak of senility which threatened it. As the Chief Justice said in his charge (paid for by the railway) to the jury: "This university will be lifted into a class all by itself, or held only by itself, and the universities of Mecca and Timbuctoo."

MY IDEAS ON ACADEMIC FREEDOM

(NOTE: *This essay was written just after I was informed that I was to be retired. Dr. Johnson once said
that for a condemned man the prospect that he was
going to be hanged must brighten up his intelligence
wonderfully. He was right.*)

―――――

EVERY now and then the subject of academic freedom
—of what things professors and students have the
right to say and to do, and what things they have
no right to say and to do—breaks out in the press.
Any new incident starts the discussion afresh. Medical
students go on a riot, or art students go on a strike,
divinity students refuse to pray, or a young lecturer
in political economy tells a Rotary Club that brokers
are crooks—and away it goes. Controversy for a time
is rife in the newspapers, till something else happens
—somebody has triplets—and it falls asleep. But the
subject is still there.

In these troubled days, when political economy has
exchanged the dust of the bookshelves for the sand of
the arena—where the young matador of the class-
room fights the bull of Capitalism—it is likely that
these disputes will multiply. This is especially the

case in Canada. We live in a divided country.

It would be greatly to be desired that we could reach some sort of general opinion on the subject. It has occurred to me that I might perform in this connection a useful service. I have now in this matter nothing to gain, nothing to lose. I have no axe to grind. The governors of McGill University have taken it from my hands and ground it blunt. Within a few short months I am to leave active work in college and to sink into the arms of the Carnegie trustees.

I would not intrude this personal information except that I wish to show at the outset that I have no further personal interest in the question of academic freedom. Nor did I ever have any, to any great extent. I have been teaching now nearly half a century, from the time when, as a teacher in training, I taught Sir Arthur Currie, a junior pupil, in the High School at Strathroy in the fall of 1888. I began work as a paid teacher in the Uxbridge High School in February, 1889. In all that time I have had only two serious matters of dispute with my employers—in Uxbridge, at the very start, when the trustees wouldn't let me go; and now at McGill, when the governors won't let me stay.

At Uxbridge I got the offer of a better job, but the trustees, merry fellows, refused to let me leave; they said that they had got me at $58.66 a month and they knew a good thing when they had it. Now the trustees of McGill, to my great surprise and much against my will, tell me that I must go. In vain I tell these rash men that this means a terrible blow to the University. They tell me, in return, that they detect in me those first symptoms of incipient senility which ravage the human brain after the age of sixty-five, but from which they themselves in the execution of their high office are fortunately exempt. They add that the application of a general rule is better than the endless disputes over individual cases; and that, when you come to think of it, is a pretty sensible argument.

So I am able to extend to these trustees that meek and insulting forgiveness which is one of the "slickest" ways that there are of getting back at people. In a short time I go from here to devote myself to the duties of another office which I have held for some years, that of President of the Anti-Mosquito Association of East Simcoe. In exchanging the service of the McGill governors for my work among the mosquitoes, I shall feel that the senility which impeded me in the one case will help greatly in the work of the other.

All this I write, designedly, in the hope that I may infuse at the start into a mean and contentious subject some atmosphere of good will.

With that, let me get to business.

People who live outside of colleges have very vague

ideas, or none at all, as to what "academic freedom" means. They know that it has a kind of hurrah to it like the "Freedom of the Seas." But it is equally mysterious. So I will say to them, in words of one syllable, what it is about. It refers first of all to the rights of students. Can they say what they like and do what they like outside the college? Can they parade the streets, break up a theatre, upset a street car? In the classroom, what can they do, and what not? Can they organize political parties, labor parties? Have they got to believe in God? What about professors? Must they believe in God? Can they talk as they like in class? What can they say out of the class? Can they take part in politics? Can they upset a street car? And what about the trustees of a college? Can they parade the streets and shout, "Rah! Rah! College Trustees!" If they give money to a college, do they get anything back or nothing? Have they bought silence? Can they stop giving it if they think their money is used in a way to injure their business, or do they have to go on giving anyway?

In the generations gone by—forty or fifty years ago—the problem of academic freedom used to centre round the question of student outbreaks which took the form of parades in the street, accompanied by wild pranks and destruction of property. Most Toronto people have heard of how the students of Varsity, years and years ago, loaded up with old boots the Russian guns that stand as Crimean trophies in the Park, and fired them off down the Avenue. Such escapades and that of the wild street parades that accompanied them, kept the police busy all night and the college faculty all day.

The situation arose out of the very dullness and severity of our student life. We had none of all the admirable dramatic activities—the writing and presentation of plays—which adorn and enrich student life today. We produced a Greek play (in Greek) once every thirty years—just as a female elephant produces offspring once in half a century. The play took three years to rehearse, three hours to represent, twenty years to forget, and ten years to revive. The rest of the time the students used to work, work, work in their little boarding-house bedrooms every night far into the night.

Then, about once every two months, they all came howling out on the street to drink beer, endless beer, about a cubic foot per student, and then go and upset a street car! Do you remember, my bygone friends of Varsity, how we used to troop down what was then Queen's Park Avenue, shouting "Caer Howell! Caer Howell!", to invade the old Caer Howell Hotel and sop up beer before looking for a street car? No, you don't, many of you; you are too far away.

All that is changed. Our students of today have not time to upset street cars. They are too busy taking

the girls out. No burning midnight oil for them
either; their game is burning gasoline. The co-eds
who sneaked into the colleges so modestly and trip-
pingly in the middle eighties have their Delilah's
vengeance. The campus Samson has lost his locks. No
street-car work for him.

But I have always thought that these student outbreaks, and any survival of them in the form of student disorder on the streets or in the theatres and
public places, should be left to the police. Outside of
the campus, a student is a citizen. If he gets arrested,
let the courts deal with him. The college has no
criminal jurisdiction over him, though the "disci-
plinary clause" of the calendar of any college sets up
a contract which permits of his expulsion. But it is
far better to leave all this alone. Let the student sit
in the police cell with a headache. Don't bail him
out. Send him a Latin grammar and a prayer book.
He'll be back presently.

Sometimes student disorder appears on a major
scale and lifts the question of academic conduct into
a first-class political and moral problem. This has
happened, still happens and is happening in the
United States, in cases that need not be cited. In
Canada, luckily, it is a long time since such a situation has arisen. But one or two cases may be cited.

An occasion in point is represented by the famous
"student rebellion" at the University of Toronto

forty years ago. The rebellion and the "general strike" in which it was expressed arose about as follows:

At that time the staff of the University of Toronto was suffering, so it was alleged, from ingrowing brains. So many of the appointments had been made from Ontario and from Toronto itself that there was a danger of over-great intellectual brilliance, like the feeding of a flame with oxygen. I think that that is a fair statement of the case. The students' paper, *Varsity*, growled with discontent. Protest and dissatisfaction were widespread. Most ill-advisedly for himself, one of the professors took up the students' cause, and took it even too far. He wrote to a Toronto newspaper a letter which turned general criticism into personal detraction.

An influential group of his own colleagues denounced him. The University put him out. The students of his faculty, nearly to a man, went on strike and refused to go to lectures. The leaders of the movement were a young man called Tucker, a poet and an idealist, long since gone; a Mr. Hamar Greenwood, now Lord Greenwood; and a William Lyon Mackenzie King, now in the Secret Service of Canada. The strike made a great commotion. There were the usual commissions of inquiries and promises by which the students were induced to go back. The professor became a farmer and lived happy ever after. In time it was all forgotten.

But I think the students made a mistake. A student has a perfect legal right to stay away from lectures and take the academic consequences. It is not like a strike of railroad employees. It is like a strike of the customers of a shop. If they had right on their side, and had all stayed away and appealed for sympathy, not force, to the people of the Province, they could have said to the College and the Legislature, "Here are our claims; sign on the dotted line." Otherwise the Legislature would have been blown up. When a bull-terrier holds a hog by the ear it doesn't let go, even if a Royal Commission is biting it at the other end. But perhaps the students were not so altogether in the right. I forget. . . . The thing, of course, couldn't happen that way in a college privately endowed. The trustees could laugh at it.

Here is another case, this time from the annals of McGill, an episode of quarter of a century ago. In the "reciprocity" election of 1911, most, but not all, of the staff were against the reciprocity policy of Sir Wilfrid Laurier. Some of us were in politics up to the neck—speaking, writing, campaigning. Most of the students, but by no means all, were on our side; the principal, strong in his devotion to an endangered empire, notoriously so. That eminent man, Mr. Clifford Sifton, was billed to speak one winter night in Montreal at the Windsor Hall. He was one of the conspicuous figures of the campaign, having broken with Sir Wilfrid, of whose Cabinet he had been a member, on the issue involved.

We—Conservatives—invited him to speak at the Students' Union before his downtown speech. We applied for permission for this to the principal. Dr. Peterson had learned in a Scottish university the art of splitting a hair. He said that the invitation was quite permissible provided we were speaking to him not as Conservatives but as individuals and that we welcomed Mr. Sifton not in any "partisan spirit" (I can still hear Dr. Peterson saying it), but as a man of eminence whom any college might be proud to honor—*et patati, et patata.*

This, of course, was just pure bunkum, a part of that glorious humbug that is to me the chief attraction of political life. But it was good enough for us. Mr. Sifton said yes. We met him with an open barouche and a students' band—not a Conservative band, just individuals who liked music. The whole of it was organized by a bulky and forceful Conservative student, Mr. John Hackett, later on the M.P. for Stanstead, in whose behalf I appealed the other day to an ungrateful electorate at Coaticook.

Mr. Sifton spoke—I don't know what he said, probably nothing—there was a crowded hall, great enthusiasm. There didn't seem to be a Liberal in sight. We thought they were all dead. We left the Union and started for the Windsor Hall, Mr. Sifton

and I and the party organizer in the barouche, a
bodyguard of "individuals" round us with torches,
and the band following behind playing, Hail, something or other.

Then all of a sudden things happened. The street
suddenly seemed to fill with Liberals, organized, we
learned after, by a large and forceful student called
Dan Gilmour, now a large and forceful lawyer and
still called Dan Gilmour. He was as big as our John
Hackett, and more noisy. The Liberal waves broke
on our parade. The band expired in a dying wail of
its trombones. Our bodyguard was thrown over the
fence. The torches were hurled all over the place. The
party organizer caught fire. The police—all French-
Canadian Laurier Liberals, understanding academic
freedom even better than Dr. Peterson—the police
stood and laughed. The students seized our carriage,
upset us in the snow, the secretary still on fire, and
took our cab up to the campus and burned it. That
was the last time I wanted to ride with a Canadian
Cabinet Minister at election time.

Now in this case everybody was wrong. It was
nonsense to say that Mr. Sifton could appear as a
non-partisan at 8 P.M. and as a raging party man at
8.30. We had no right to the premises, and no right
to use the name of McGill. They had no right to put
us in the snow and to set our organizer on fire, nor
to use the campus for burning a Conservative cab.

The occasion was only saved by the undercurrent of decent feeling and by the idea of not invoking law or making trouble. It was a queer mixture of academic freedom and the worst of it. . . . And in any case we won the election.

But the one serious problem of students' freedom today is that of what they may write or not write in their student newspapers. I was going to say, with an old man's impatience, in their *everlasting* newspapers. Why can't they still be content to write on such things as "The Birthplace of Homer," "Was Shakespeare at his best as a Dramatist or a Metallurgist?" "Ode to Canada," and that sort of beautiful stuff that never broke the sleep of a trustee? But, no! they must write on such subjects as the C.C.F. and the rights of students to belong to the Liberal Party, and whether the college staff ought to be fired, and they announce the formation of a Russian Soviet in the basement of the Arts Building.

What should be done about all that? I don't know. I have no idea. It's an insoluble problem. If such writing breaks the law of the land, then let the law of the land look after it. But it doesn't. It merely brings the name of the college into disrepute by its use in the title of the paper, and means loss of students, loss of fees, discredit and lowered status.

Sue the students for damages? They have no money. Students never realize that, if they print and circulate a paper, calling it, let us say, *The McGill University This-or-That*, they are appropriating an asset of honor and reputation and worth which it has taken better men than themselves a hundred years to create. They might just as well ask to take the McGill bank account. Any students who want to use the college name should submit to the college censorship. More still. Students are rarely content to express their views in the form of a letter signed humbly and properly, "John Smith." Their own insignificance defeats them. They want to write it *editorially*, as if they wielded the thunder of a London *Times:* "We think this," and "We incline to believe that." Do we? I incline to think that "we" have a touch of megalomania about us.

But for all that—nothing. The best policy is to give the absolutely greatest possible measure of freedom; let it all alone; don't see it. If it reaches a point —in dirtiness, let us say—that is intolerable, then throw the offending student out so far that he will never be found again; if possible, get him sent to jail on a criminal charge. But never act till the point where every fair-minded parent or fellow student— even the college girls—are on your side.

All these problems in academic freedom are, however, of less import in Canada just now than the problem of the professor. Where does *his* liberty begin and end? How big a fool can he be? To discuss it fully would need a volume. As Virgil puts it in his own neat way, *"Longum est"*—it would take all night. But the key to it is perhaps to be found in this simple idea: A professor reduced to his lowest terms is a person engaged under a contract to do certain things at certain times and in certain places. If he does something else instead, he is not fulfilling his contract. But, equally, if he does other things elsewhere, he is not violating his contract.

No great difficulty arises in the case of professors moored in the safe and secluded anchorage of Mathematics or Philology. They write and think as they please. A recent treatise by my colleague, Professor Sullivan, was called by the mathematical reviews a "daring book." But he never got arrested. Biology, outside of Tennessee, is pretty safe, and even Divinity, that used to be the battleground of academic freedom, is now only a "historic site." It doesn't matter now if a professor says that Adam was a baboon, and that the six "days" of creation were really six aeons of eternity—make it longer if you like. The students will only yawn and the parents wish that the professor would get down to something practical.

But turn to such subjects as political economy, and the scene changes: It is like leaving the stillness of a great cave for the noise and tumult of a market place. Political Economy is the "ugly sister" of Arts— a mean, snarling virago, living on quarrels and controversy; utterly different from the reverend senility of Philosophy—right out of Noah's Ark, the chattering femininity of Languages and the cold severity of Mathematics, lit only by the Aurora Borealis.

Hence it comes that just now, in Canada and in the United States, the question of Academic Freedom is focused in the direction of politics, political activity and political belief. Can a professor be a member of the C.C.F.? Can he make a speech (outside of his college) in which he attacks the institution of banking, declares that bankers in "creating credit" are robbing society of the money power which society creates? Can he say that he does not think that a poor man ought to have his shirt taxed to pay wages and dividends for a textile company?

Personally, I don't see why not. Whether these propositions are or are not sound has nothing to do with the case. Personally, I don't think that they are. It is true that a banker creates credit with his left hand and lends it with his right; but he can't create it for himself. He only gets the interest—a *quid pro quo* for what he does. I think that if the Government takes over the function of banking it will make a terrible mess of it. We shall see Comrade Abervitch and his fellows handing out free loans like free lunch. So with the tariff tax on a poor man's shirt, though there, perhaps, the economic theory is not quite so obvious. I saw into it very clearly while I was on the pay-roll of McGill, but it is getting a little dim now.

In fact it seems to me very easy in principle to state exactly what the academic freedom of a professor means, although it is no doubt not always easy to apply the principle to a particular case. A professor, when talking or writing outside of his university and on occasions and in publications not connected with his work, ought to have exactly the same rights and be under exactly the same limitations as any other citizen. If he violates the law, the law is there to punish him.

He ought not on such occasions to make an unfair use of the name of his college, or imply in any way that he is speaking for the college. But it is inevitable that other people will refer to him as a professor, and refer to his college to indicate where he comes from and who and what he is. This is well within his rights. If I publish a book on Political Economy in New York, I have the right to sign the title-page Stephen Leacock, McGill University, because that tells people where to find me. But when I leave McGill it ceases to be an address and I shall never use it again.

When a professor is talking in his classroom, that is a different matter. He is then talking under a contract, and what he can properly say or not say depends entirely on the terms of his contract. If he is lecturing in a college owned and conducted by a church, the matter is simple, because he understands from the start that he is there to expound the doctrine taught by the church; if not, he ought not to be there. What these doctrines are he can easily find out.

But when a college is run by a board of trustees the matter is not so simple. The professor is there to teach exactly what he is hired to teach, but it is hard for him to find this out. If he is told to teach political economy, there are as many kinds of political economy as there are kinds of trustees. All that can be done in such a case is for the professor to explain as well as he can the pro and con of everything reasonably included in the work; to indicate sources of information; to express, if he likes, his own opinion, but only as his opinion, and never to embark on the form of partisan persuasion called propaganda.

Thus—to give a personal illustration—it was my pleasant duty a few years ago to teach in my class a distinguished young Japanese feudal prince. It was my duty to teach him political economy. It would have been grossly wrong of me to try to convert him, in my classroom, to Christianity or to persuade him that Adam was not a baboon.

There is, and is bound to be, a great deal of social unrest in the colleges. It is part of the hard times; and in the colleges the young men contrast their own energy and industry and the financial sacrifices they make with the fact that they go out of college to stand idle in the market place, without a job, without a chance. It is a great shame, and if the world cannot remedy it within a reasonable term, the world of today will go down. All of this is inevitable. The teaching of professors has nothing to do with it. It is life.

Nor does the average student take stock necessarily in everything and anything that professors say. They live in a world of books and talk and discussion. They have easy access to everything printed, revolutionary or conservative. They are not stampeded this way or that, by a few catchwords. The bogey of socialism which frightens college trustees, and makes them turn toward persecution, has no effect on students. Mainly they are concerned with their own lives, their own hopes and fears, their own prospects, and often the *res angusta domi* of their own people at home, whom they hope to help with money when they can.

Leave such students alone and all is wholesome: College trustees in general do not realize how easily we get on in the classrooms, how little friction, how much interest. But if and when the trustees and governors come and stand at the door like jailers, ready to use the unrestrained power which they possess, then they turn the professors into dumb, silent, obedient figures, doing what is demanded because they dare not face dismissal—and the students into sullen rebels, ready to join any political party which proposes to fight rich men.

If we do not get, or achieve, better times in the next five years or so, if this cruel situation is to last, then inevitably this country will, in sheer despair and discontent, vote into public power exactly such people as have been described. When they get into power, when they become the Prime Ministers and Cabinets of Canada and of its provinces, then they will find their programme as impossible of practical realization as socialisms always are. In the long run, only truth prevails. What these people advocate is not possible; it is a mere soap bubble; it is born in the generous visions of youth.

Once in power, these visionaries will find it necessary to stop looking into their kaleidoscope. They cannot do the vast vague things they dreamed of doing; not in a world of sinners. They will not "socialize" all money, "debank" the banks and "distariff" the tariff. Their reforms will be as long in coming as the Greek kalends and the Alberta Social Credit. But meantime they will be in power; and, being only human, they will be inclined to deal with the colleges and the college trustees as these have dealt with them. Let the trustee reflect, if he knows Latin, *Hodie tibi: cras mihi.*

Which raises the question of trustees themselves. What about their academic freedom?

There is often so much talk about the academic

freedom of professors that people are apt to forget that there is, or ought to be, in equal measure an academic freedom of the trustees or governors of a university. In the case of boards of trustees or governors who merely act as the deputies of a legislature, no particular difficulty arises. But it is otherwise with the trustees of an institution supported by private endowment, and the case becomes extreme when an institution is supported in whole or in part by the annual contributions of the trustees themselves.

It is surely only fair that they need not give their money unless they want to. It is scarcely possible for them to ask to get back what they have already given. But they are entitled, in all justice, to say that they won't give any more. If they feel that the things taught, or the manner of teaching, in the college injures their business, they may say that either such teaching has got to stop or they won't give any more money. For example, if they think that Mr. Brown's lectures on Kant's *Critique of Pure Reason* drive their customers crazy and hurt retail business, they are entitled to tell Mr. Brown to cut it out or let the college take the consequences. If a governor of a college is a stock broker and he says that he doesn't want the Mathematical Department to take up the Theory of Probability because it would give his profession away, he is on perfectly fair ground.

Or if a governor feels that as a banker he wishes all

reference to banking suppressed; or that as a manu-
facturer he does not want the consumer mentioned
—these men are also on perfectly fair ground. They
are not saying that the college must not teach these
things, but only that it must not teach them with
their money. I cannot conceive anything more logical.

The heroic answer at once suggests itself that money
is not worth having at that price. But in reality those
who would protest most loudly, the professoriate,
would not be prepared to face the consequences of
their protest. Suppose it were said to them: "Now,
my dear sirs, if Mr. Brown insists on discussing Kant,
and if the Economics Department keep on referring
to the consumer, it will cost you a thirty per cent re-
duction in your salaries. You may choose for your-
selves. These gentlemen pay the piper, or part of the
piper, and they propose to call the tune, or at least
some of the notes." In plain actual fact, in the brutal
world we live in, the professors themselves, with their
homes to keep and their children to send to school,
would be the first to suppress the lectures.

Now we might say that if the trustees were far-
sighted men, they would not impose such restrictions.
But that is quite another matter. Suppose they do?
There is no answer to it. They needn't give unless they
want to. The truth is that any college which falls
into the unhappy position of living on the current
bounty of rich men finds itself in chains. The chains

may be lightly bound and never tightened, may be worn perhaps with little realization that they are there—but there they are, just the same. It is a situation in which the idea of academic freedom must be put aside and replaced by the idea of academic tolerance. The difference is the same as religious freedom under an Act of Toleration, and religious freedom under a Constitution.

But, fortunately, for most professors in most colleges most of the time, these difficulties do not arise. The professors teach their Conic Sections, and their Latin Irregular Verbs year after year, without knowing that these sections are only conic and these verbs are only irregular as long as the trustees wish to have them called so. Many of them no doubt have had, though for a shorter time, the same pleasant experience that has been my lot: The years passing one by one, and ten by ten, till they have reached out for more than the third of a century, without a jar, without a word of reprimand from the trustees, till at the end, to my utter surprise, they told me to go—a piece of academic playfulness of which the joke is all on me.

I'LL STAY IN CANADA

(NOTE: *This article was written at the suggestion of an English editor who asked whether I should not come "home" to England [where I was born] now that I have finished my work at McGill University. The wide circulation and the very kind reception that the article received encourage me to reproduce it as the closing chapter of this book.*)

YOU are kind enough to suggest that I might, being now free from work, come home to England. But no, no, don't tempt me. It wouldn't work. I know it wouldn't. It sounds fine. But there are all kinds of difficulties, things you wouldn't think of at first— questions of language and manners; a lot of them. Honestly, I don't think I'd better try it.

You see, it's been sixty years, this early spring, since I came out from England as a little boy of six, so wise that I knew all about the Trojan War and which Gods fought for which side, and so ignorant that I had never seen a bark canoe or a bob-sleigh and didn't know what a woodchuck was. We crossed the Atlantic, which I recall as continuous ice; were in river steamers for four days; then in a train with a

284

queer little engine that threw hemlock sparks all over the bush; and then thirty miles in a lumber wagon—and we were *there*.

After that my brothers and I never saw a railway train again for three years, till someone built a railway to Lake Simcoe and the "cars" came. There followed another three years, and then we went away to school and to the world. But the "stamp" I carry is that of the farm in Georgina Township and my predilection is for the soil and the Canadian bush. Forever, I like the sunrise.

I worked at teaching. I taught for three months, in training, eighteen years old, at the old Strathroy High School with General Sir Arthur Currie, our greatest Canadian, as my pupil.

Then I taught for a year at Uxbridge High School. Then I taught ten years at Upper Canada College. Then I got quite a good job at McGill University and held it for thirty-five years. My life has been as simple as one of Xenophon's Marches. But at least my jobs grew longer. The next, I think, will be what you'd call permanent.

But now, as you say, I am free to do as I please; and, if I like, after sixty years I could come "home." Certainly it sounds tempting. Yet, as I say, there are difficulties. The first is the question of language. When I left Hampshire I spoke English. But I've lost it, and it might be too late to pick it up again. You

see, we speak differently here. I don't mean unedu-
cated people, I mean educated men, like my friends at
my club (The University Club, Montreal—you can't
miss it; it's just opposite McGill University).

We used to be ashamed of our Canadian language,
before the war, and try to correct it and take on English phrases and say, "What a ripping day," instead
of "What a peach of a morning," and "Ah you thah?"
instead of "Hullo Central," and "Oh, rather!" instead
of "O-Hell-yes." But now, since the Great War put
Canada right on a level with the Portuguese and the
Siamese and those fellows who came from—ah! one
forgets the names, but it doesn't matter—I mean,
made Canada a real nation—we just accept our own
language and are not ashamed of it. We say "yep!"
when we mean "yep!" and don't try to make out it's
"yes," which is a word we don't use; and if we mean
"four" we say so and don't call it "faw."

So you see, there's the question of language. Then
there's the difference of education. I don't mean that
we are not educated—us fellers in the University
Club—because we are: only in a different way. At
first sight you English people would not think we
were educated because we learned different things.
Any member of the club knows what a kilowatt is,
and you don't; but on the other hand, our members
would think that a "perfect aorist" is either a vacuum
cleaner or an Italian trombone player.

It is just that difference. I remember a few years ago a distinguished English bishop, speaking at our club, said that he felt that Greek had practically made him what he was; we felt exactly the same about him and thought it very manly and British of him to admit it straight out.

Then, there's the question of manners. There it would be pretty hard for me or for any of my friends here to "get by." You see, we are not just quite what you call gentlemen. Not quite. In the dark and if we don't talk, you could hardly tell us. But when we begin to feel easy and at home the thing comes out. I don't just know what it consists of: I think we are a little too unrestrained and we have a way of referring to money, a thing of which you never definitely speak in England.

I remember, in making conversation with that bishop, I asked him if his salary went right on while he was out here, and when he said, "I beg your pardon," all I could say was, "Forget it." Of course, the bishop didn't know that in Canada we never feel at ease with a man till we know what his salary is, and which of the gold mines he bought shares in last.

All this means we lack "class." There isn't a sufficient distinction between us and those lower down in money. Personally I can go bass fishing with a taxi driver and a Toronto surgeon and an American tourist and the "feller that rents the boat" and can't see any difference. Neither can they. There isn't any.

That brings me to the Americans! There's another reason for not wanting to leave Canada for England. I'd hate to be so far away from the United States. You see, with us it's second nature, part of our lives, to be near them. Every Sunday morning we read the New York funny papers, and all week we read about politics in Alabama and Louisiana, and whether they caught the bandits that stole the vault of the national bank, and—well, you know American news—there's no other like it. And the Americans come-and-go up here, and we go-and-come down there, and they're educated just as we are and know all about kilowatts but quit Latin at the fourth declension.

Their colleges are like ours and their clubs are like ours and their hotels are like ours and Rotaries and Lions and Kiwanis like ours. Honestly, you can't tell where you are unless you happen to get into a British Empire Society; and anyway, they have those in Boston and in Providence, and the Daughters of the American Revolution is practically a British organization—so all that is fifty-fifty.

Our students go and play hockey with their stoodents and our tourists going out meet their towrists coming in. The Americans come up here and admire us for the way we hang criminals. They sit in our club and say, "You certainly do hang them, don't you!" My! they'd like to hang a few! The day may be coming when they will. Meantime, we like to hang people to make the Americans sit up.

And in the same way we admire the Americans for the way they shovel up mountains and shift river-courses and throw the map all round the place. We sit in the club, fascinated, and listen to an American saying, "The proposal is to dam up the Arkansas River and make it run backward over the Rockies." That's the stuff! That's conversation.

There you are again—conversation. It would be hard for me or any Canadian to learn to "converse" in England. You see, English conversation turns upon foreign politics and international affairs. It runs to such things as—"But don't you think that the Singapore Base would have been better if it had been at Rangoon or at least on the Irrawaddy?" "Ah, but would that really control Hoopow, or, for that matter, Chefoo?"

Now, we don't talk about that. Listen to us in my club and you hear, "He told me that in Central Patricia they were down to the second level and that there was enough stuff *right in sight* to make it a cinch. I bought 100 at 2.30 and yesterday it had got to three dollars. . . ."

That's real talk. And that's our country, anyway— our unfailing interest, for all of us, in its vast development, its huge physical future. In this last sixty years—since I've known it—we have filled it in and filled it in like a huge picture lying in a frame from the frozen seas to the American line, from Nova Scotia to the Pacific. What the English feel about the Armada and the Scottish about Bannockburn, the Canadian, consciously or not, feels about the vast geography of Canada.

There is something inspiring in this building of a new country in which even the least of us has had some part. I can remember how my father went— from our Lake Simcoe farm—to the first Manitoba boom of over fifty years ago—before the railway. He had an idea that what the West needed was British energy and pluck. He came back broke in six months. Then Uncle Edward went; he had a gifted mind and used to quote to us that "the Star of the Empire glitters in the West." He did better. He came back broke only after four years.

Then my brothers Dick and Jim went. Dick was in the Mounted Police and then worked in a saloon and came home broke. Jim got on fine but he played poker too well and had to leave terribly fast. Charlie and George and Teddy went—they all went but me. I was never free to go till now, but I may start at any time. Going West, to a Canadian, is like going after the Holy Grail to a knight of King Arthur. All Canadian families have had, like mine, their Western Odyssey.

It's the great spaces that appeal. To all of us here, the vast unknown country of the North, reaching away to the polar seas, supplies a peculiar mental background. I like to think that in a few short hours in a train or car I can be in the primeval wilderness of the North; that if I like, from my summer home, an hour or two of flight will take me over the divide and down to the mournful shores of the James Bay, untenanted till yesterday, now haunted with its flock of airplanes hunting gold in the wilderness. I never have gone to the James Bay; I never go to it; I never shall. But somehow I'd feel lonely without it.

No, I don't think I can leave this country. There is something in its distances and its isolation and its climate that appeal forever. Outside my window as I write in the dark of early morning—for I rise like a farm hand—the rotary snow ploughs on the Côte des Neiges Road are whirling in the air the great blanket of snow that buried Montreal last night. To the north, behind the mountain, the Northern Lights blink on a thousand miles of snow-covered forest and frozen rivers.

We are "sitting pretty" here in Canada. East and west are the two oceans far away; we are backed up against the ice cap of the pole; our feet rest on the fender of the American border, warm with a hundred years of friendship. The noise and tumult of Europe we scarcely hear—not for us the angers of the Balkans, the weeping of Vienna and the tumults of Berlin. Our lot lies elsewhere—shoveling up mountains, floating in the sky to look for gold, and finding still the Star of Empire in the West.

Thank you, Mother England, I don't think I'll "come home." I'm "home" now. Fetch me my carpet slippers from the farm. I'll rock it out to sleep right here.

Punch E. Wilson
Sophomore
Fall - 1949